INTERNATIONAL POLITICS

HER MAJESTY'S EMPIRE: A STUDY OF THE CONTROL AND MANIPULATION OF THE UNITED STATES BY BRITAIN.

BY

M.F. ONUCHUKWU

ISBN: 9781707061860

To
My Creator,
I give thanks for according me the privilege to write this book. From Him, I draw the divine wisdom, strength and courage to execute this beautiful masterpiece.

Preface.

The reader of the book must take him time to thoroughly understand the first eight chapters of the book. They form the basic foundation for the whole write up. Failure to adhere to this instruction, shall lead to a very poor understanding of the analysis done in the remaining seven chapters of the book.

The reader must also acquaint himself or herself prior to the study of the book with the narratives of the various coup d'états that the United States CIA had participated in during her existence. The author doesn't want the reader to limit himself or herself to just the coup d'états used in writing the book. The more the number of the narratives of the coup d'état the United States CIA has been involved in that the reader knows and understands, the greater the likelihood the reader will appreciate the analysis done in the book.

The author employs a rhetoric that's easy to understand throughout the entire book; the reason being to ensure that the reader's understanding of the subject matter being discussed is improved greatly.

Contents.

15 – Conclusions; A New United States Foreign Policy?

Predation; Parasitism – Chapter One

A predator can be defined as an organism that lives by feeding on other organisms. The other organisms it feeds on are called its prey. A predator has what we may term as "predatory characteristics".

Predation may be defined as any relationship between two organisms (the organism can be a simple or complex one) where primal energy flows from one organism to the other. The organism that loses energy and vitality is the prey whereas the organism that gains primal energy and vitality is the predator.

A parasite can be defined as any living thing that relates with another living thing (host) by feeding on the vitality of the living thing it relates with. By their nature, parasites live because of the nutrients they get from feeding on their hosts. The moment a host stops existing, the parasite tends to find another host or dies a natural death. The effect a parasite has on a host is always very harmful no matter how little or how big the nutrition it derives from the host is. In most cases, the feeding leads to the death of a host. A parasite never benefits its host.

A parasite can either feed directly or indirectly on the vitality of its host. A host which the parasite feeds on directly is a PRIMARY host whereas a host through which the parasite feeds on another host is called a SECONDARY host. A secondary host is often used by a parasite to switch from one primary host to another primary host. It often acts as an intermediary between the parasite and the primary host.

A parasite is a type of predator. It is a predator because it feeds on its host like a predator will feed on its prey. A parasite will always possess predatory behavioral characteristics that enable it to survive in nature. There are two main behavioral characteristics of which most natural predators and preys possess. These characteristics are camouflage and mimicry. They can be used by both for offensive and defensive purposes. The predators employ them for offensive purposes while the preys use them for defensive purposes.

The basic behavioral mechanics of a parasite isn't complex. It is a very simple one. The foundational simplicity of such mechanics makes it very effective in usage. This may be the reason why the British government adopted it in the first place as a model for its foreign policy responses.

It is also very important that we defined what a parasite is because it will certainly aid our understanding of particular facts about Her Majesty's government written in the subsequent chapters of this book. A good understanding of the nature of parasitism will help any reader understand why and how British government's activities have been more harmful than beneficial to all the nations of the world.

Camouflage – Chapter Two

In Chapter One, we clearly stated that camouflage was a predatory characteristic. In nature, most predators employ this characteristic in an attacking ot defending manner. You may be wondering what the word camouflage means; it simply means to hide or conceal an object (including living and non-living things).

Camouflage is very important for the survival of predators. A predator must deceive its prey. It must blend into its surroundings and assume the form of its surroundings to make a prey feel at ease in such a surrounding. Predators understand that preys will always activate their flight mode in dangerous environments and this behavior is only but a survival mechanism. Therefore, predators are good at camouflaging their presence to a prey. Once the prey loses its guard, they attack him with viciousness.

All predators survive through feeding to obtain their needed nutrition as well as mating to reproduce their kind. The instinct to feed is primal just like the instinct to mate. Life ensures that every living thing is endowed with these characteristics no matter how attenuated. The primal energy though it cannot be seen seeks to destroy and create. The process of this destruction and creation is cyclical as can be seen in the cycle of life and death.

Predation favors predators and disfavors preys. It must be noted that both predators and preys use camouflage to survive. In most cases, the prey develops both simple and complex behavioral mechanisms of camouflage to deal with the predator's camouflaging behaviors. This is very natural. The preys must devise a way to survive and the predators must devise ways to outsmart the predators and devise ways to derive nutrition from them.

The nature of predation is in itself very complex and camouflage aids it a great deal. From the least complex organisms to humans, we observe how camouflage helps survival instincts.

A good understanding of camouflage is also needed, so that the reader can appreciate the concept of camouflage and how the British government has employed it in expanding her Empire across the world. This understanding will also enable the reader to appreciate why and how Her Majesty's government employed such behavioral mechanisms in her foreign policy.

Mimicry – Chapter Three

Mimicry is another predatory behavioral characteristic. Mimicry can be explained when you consider that organisms (both simple and complex) have certain behavioral patterns. However, it is always possible for an organism to behave like another organism of a different nature from itself in order to feed on (if a prey) or protect (if a predator) itself from that organism. The more complex an organism becomes, the more difficult it becomes to copy or imitate the behavior of the organism.

Mimicry, though a predatory behavioral mechanism, is nature's way of proving its oneness. It is nature's way of showing that the same primal energy with its distinct attributes permeates all things in existence. Mimicry gives organisms the power to imitate other organisms' movement, speech, appearance, odor and other signals specific to the other organism's survival behavioral mechanisms.

The purpose of mimicry is to increase the predatory chances of a predator as well as the escape chances of the prey. Mimicry tends to ensure that both predator and prey doesn't become extinct on the evolutionary scale of life. What this means is that, the copying or imitation of mating and feeding instincts across different species of organisms, allows organisms to be preyed upon as well as to be predators in their own ways.

From the perspective of predation (if you consider both preys and predators), predators who imitate the behaviors of their prey increase to a very large extent their chances of feeding on the prey. The prey becomes grossly unaware of the threat it faces and puts down its defensive mechanism. The same goes for preys that copy the behavioral mechanisms of the predators of the species of organisms that predates on them, they tend to survive in an environment full of the predators of their own species.

It is very important that the reader thoroughly grasps the nature of mimicry. As always, a good understanding of what mimicry entails will go a long way to aid the understanding of Her Majesty's government and her relations with other nations of the world. This understanding will lead to the true appreciation of the magnanimity of what shall be revealed in the remaining chapters of this great book.

An effort shall be made to reconcile subject matter with the examples that will be laid down to give the reader a broader perspective on the British government's predatory behavior across the globe.

Octopus; Polypus – Chapter Four

An octopus is a sea creature (has brains and eyes) with a soft body, and eight long (flexi-extendable) tentacles. Two of the tentacles are used for walking while the remaining six are used to feed. This definition of an octopus quickly gives us an idea of the nature of an octopus. If you take away the eight long arms of the octopus, it ceases to be an octopus, it becomes another thing entirely. The main feature differentiating an octopus from other sea creatures with flexi-extendable arms is that it has eight flexi-extendable tentacles.

The Octopus belongs to the family of organisms (Polypus) whose main characteristics are their multi-tentacles and venomous nature. It's important that we mention the other characteristics of the octopus as pertains to its nature. The characteristic of the octopus includes: (i) Octopuses feed on crustaceans like crab by injecting them with paralyzing saliva using its tentacles with sucker appendages. (ii) Octopuses feed on shelled molluscs by forcing their shell apart, or by drilling a hole in the shell to inject a nerve toxin. (iii) The sucker appendages allow the octopus to attach itself to the prey (host) and manipulate it.

Most octopuses can camouflage. This makes them predators. They carry out this camouflage by the expulsion of inks from their ink sacs. The ink expelled from the ink sac conceals the octopus and gives it enough time for it to escape. The octopus also has the ability to blend into its surroundings. It does this by attaching itself to the rocks located at the bottom of the sea and changing its color patterns to match those of the rocks. A prey approaching the octopus in such an environment, will not notice the presence of the octopus until it gets caught in the octopus's web of tentacles.

The octopuses also have the ability to mimic. When an octopus senses danger, it can behave like a bigger and more threatening predator to a potential predator by stretching out its tentacles to magnify its appearance. The rapid change in appearance also allows an octopus to deceive its preys as well as its predators. It does this by changing its colors to appear like an organism that's very undesirable in appearance to a potential predator.

The need to understand how the octopus is structured and functions can't be overemphasized. It is important that the reader thoroughly grasps all the facts written about the polypus. It shall aid his understanding of the subsequent chapters of the book. The octopus is the ideal creature that represents British government activities in the world. The British government acts exactly like a polypus when it comes to dealing with other nations of the world. Her Majesty's government has mastered the art of predating like a polypus.

Empire – Chapter Five

An empire can be defined as a number of individual nations that are ruled (controlled) by the government of one particular country. It is made up of a group of states or countries ruled over by a single monarch (usually a king or a queen). An empire is a sovereign state that functions as a collection of nations (people making up the nation) that are ruled over by an emperor or empress.

An empire is imperialistic in posture. Empires always adopt the policy of extending their influence over other foreign nations. They accomplish such feats by using forceful control and manipulative methods. Imperialism is the main ingredient of an empire's foreign policy. The Empire possesses what we can term as a "psychology of supremacy". The psychology of supremacy is in itself based on an overestimation of the Empire's abilities. It is basically rooted in pride. Imperialism dictates to a large extent the formal and informal political, social, cultural and economic directions of indigenous populations where the imperialist control.

An Empire more often than not, formulates policies that encourage the acquisition of full or partial political control another country, occupying such a country with settlers and exploiting it economically. This may be termed as colonialism. The colonialist mentality of Empires can also be attributed to the "psychology of supremacy". The false sense of infallibility of a colonialist government drives her to expand her influence and control over other territories that doesn't belong to them. The idea behind colonialism is for the colonialist government to dominate the indigenous peoples of the territories being colonized, to impose their ways of life on them and pursue their own economic selfish interests.

The policies of Empires always encourage the widening of the politico-socio-economic gap between the empire and the foreign nations it exerts control and influence over. The consolidation of the gains of an Empire comes from what you may term as globalization. The power of an Empire is cemented when her influence on the process of interaction and integration amongst the people and government is expanded. The greater the global interactions amongst nations it controls, the easier it is for the Empire to exert control over them. This becomes more effective when there are substantial advances in the transportation and communication technology. Globalization promotes the rapid acculturation of the nations ruled by the Empire.

It is important for the reader to understand what an Empire is. A good understanding of the nature of an Empire shall go a long way to aid the reader in grasping how Her Majesty's government runs her empire.

Divide and Rule ("By Forcing Their Shell Apart") – Chapter Six

To divide means to separate something (usually an object) into separate parts. Division leads to the splitting up of the constituent parts of an object(s). Most things can be divided into different parts. When we divide, we tend to pull apart the whole. Division is applicable to almost anything in nature. In human affairs, it is possible to separate groups, to pull them apart or to split them. More often than not, people tend to disagree amongst themselves about certain issues in life. They cannot agree on particular ideas because they seem not to understand how those things should be as dictated by nature. They erroneously imagine how these things should be. These false ideas lead to disagreement. These disagreements on ideas (ideologies) could act as points where division takes off. A potential enemy can exploit these divisive weaknesses to their own profit.

In groups, when people are divided, it's easy to further divide and control them. It's much easier to rule over them. To rule means to have control over a group of people. To gain control over people, there must be a way to divide them. To gain control over a group of people is to separate them based on certain ideas they nurture. Usually they are separated based on those ideas which they fail to understand properly. The failure to properly interpret those ideas which tear groups apart will remain an Achilles heel to the group in question. Those persons, who gain control over other groups, gain these controls by exploiting the dividing factors amongst them. The key questions a ruler may ask are: How does the group differ? Why does the group differ? A ruler who possesses a proper understanding of the dynamics of a group creates points of division or differences between them and shall rule them with ease.

To divide and rule is to control people by exploiting where they disagree, keeping those disagreements on course and ensuring that such disagreements lead to conflicts when necessary. The most intelligent of groups often find these things in common and use them to affect the groups which they seek to control. Divide and rule is effective in settings where the ruler seeks to exploit a group for political, social, economic and cultural purposes.

Her Majesty's government runs her empire on this very principle of divide and rule. A principle, which I believe was learnt from the Roman Empire. An Emperor or Empress seeks to establish and expand his/her empire and wouldn't mind doing so at the expense of its subject. A proper understanding of this subject matter shall indeed aid the reader in grasping properly the contents of the remaining chapters of this book.

Corruption ("To Inject A Nerve Toxin") – Chapter Seven

A nerve toxin is any kind of poison that affects the nervous system. In Chapter four, you read that an octopus kills its prey by injecting it with a nerve toxin. A nerve toxin when injected into the circulatory system of a prey by an octopus has the ability to paralyze it quickly. The nerve toxin by nature is poisonous because it inhibits the transmission of impulses across neural pathways. A prey that's injected with this lethal dose of nerve toxin can die immediately.

The nervous system of any organism is the complexities of neural pathways that allow the organism to receive specific impulses from its environment and respond to them in a effective manner. A nervous system is important to an organism because without the nervous system, the organism wouldn't be aware of what goes on in the environment. A damaged nervous system means a corrupted awareness. Organisms with damaged nervous systems wouldn't know how to respond in a hostile environment or to a predator. They quickly surrender to the whims and caprices of the predator.

Corruption is act of making somebody behave in an immoral, illegal or dishonest manner. Corruption makes somebody change his or her behaviors from the original way that it was meant to be to a more immoral, illegal and dishonest way. Corruption is harmful in its own ways. Corruption in a governmental system may be likened to a nerve toxin in the nervous system, especially when you compare the poisonous effects both have on the systems they are injected into. Corruption in government is like poison in an organism. When effectively utilized, corruption can damage and paralyze any government which oversees a group of people. Corruption tends to be very aggressive when there's something to be gained through the corruption.

A group of people when poisoned with corruption act in immoral or illegal or dishonest ways, more often than not they act in ways detrimental to their own society. To corrupt an individual in government, an enemy may adopt ways like enticing him with money, women or higher political position. Money and sex remains one of the most effective weapons of corrupting a society. From wads of cash to pornography to bribery to injustice to absolute power, the many ways of corrupting a group of people increasingly becomes very complex when you consider the different complex behavioral archetypes that make up the group. Corruption when effectively managed can be a strategy of promoting division amongst groups in a society. Nothing paralyzes a society as fast as corruption. It is damning.

It is important that the reader gets also good grasp of what this particular chapter lays out on corruption. Her Majesty's government has employed corruption as a nerve toxin that paralyzes the societies where she seeks to govern in ways quicker than anything ever imagined; and her nerve toxin of corruption is indeed virulent. Like a polypus, the British government through her tentacles (via the sucker appendages) poisons other nations she seeks to dominate with corruption. These nations die a natural death as time progresses.

The British MI6 – Chapter Eight

The British MI6 (also known as the British Foreign Office) is saddled with the responsibility of gathering foreign intelligence for Her Majesty's government. The British MI6 can gather intelligence through humans (HUMINT), signals (SIGINT), open source (OPINT), etc. However, the activities of the British MI6 like most intelligence organizations in the world extend way more than gathering foreign intelligence. It includes spreading of political propaganda, economic sabotage, assassinations, smear campaigns, etc. The web of activities of the British MI6 affects in so many ways the political, social, cultural and economic aspects of the different nations of the world.

In defining an octopus, we had earlier said that it had brains and eyes. The brains and eyes of the octopus allow it to learn through observation, perceive its environment, control its tentacles and give definite responses. You may compare the British MI6 with the brains and eyes of an octopus. The British MI6 acts as the brains and eyes of the Her Majesty's government. She's always there watching, planning and strategizing on how to spread its tentacles. The British MI6 has so many characteristics, of which it is important that the reader understands before we proceed to the remaining chapters of this book.

The British MI6 has its own officers (staff). By officers, we mean the men and women that are formally employed by the British MI6 to carry out certain delegated duties on behalf of the British MI6 organization. These intelligence officers may pose as diplomats of the countries where they are assigned to work. More often than not, they are given minimized duties to enable them have time to carry out their intelligence work. The officers of the British MI6 may be graduates or not. They may be recruited basically from anywhere on planet earth which may include universities, the British armed forces (the British MI6 likes to recruit ex-SAS officers) and the British police, etc. The officers of the British MI6 are always stationed both home and abroad. They can be assigned to work in any continent and country of the world. The British MI6 may undergo a purge from time to time. By purge, I mean a massive sack of the existing pool of staff and replacement with another pool of staff.

The British MI6 has the ability to conduct operations. The operations conducted by the British MI6 may range from gathering foreign intelligence to spreading political propaganda to economic sabotage to recruiting foreign spies. The British MI6 operations are usually very complex and tend to encompass broader activities that underline an expanding empire.

The British MI6 has her agents scattered all over the world. An agent of the British MI6 may be defined as one whose informal connections (direct or indirect) with the organizations make him or her act (knowingly or unknowingly) in the interest of Her Majesty's government. The British MI6 has a dossier for all her agents. The dossier contains the professional abilities of the agents, their personalities and under what circumstances they should be activated and used. The British MI6 also recruits professional criminals as British MI6 agents.

The British MI6 can exert control over a group. It is possible to have the British MI6 control a group of persons. The British MI6 may infiltrate any group, corrupt it and then split it apart. This way it gains control over such a group using its agents in that group.

The British MI6 has her headquarters in London. At this headquarter; she has "regional" desks from where she communicates with field officers who in turn gives them feedback as to the activities taking place in the regions where they operate.

The British MI6 has a director who oversees the day to day running of the organization. The British MI6 also has a chief, whose duty is to head the organization. He overlooks the daily handling relations and liaison with other departments of the British government. The chief also gives final clearance for foreign operations.

The British MI6 has stations and sub-stations located in different countries of the world. These stations maybe located inside or outside the embassies of the countries where they are located. The stations are charged with recruiting spies in the countries where they are located. They also monitor and gather intelligence on the various diplomats residing in the country where they are located.

The British MI6 also runs training centers. At these training centers, they give instructions and practices to their officers and direct agents on escape and evasion, sabotage, demolition, outdoor pursuits, surveillance and interrogation.

The British MI6 also thrives on what we may term "in-situ" residents. These residents are usually long term expatriates residing in the country where the British MI6 has her interests. The job of the in-situ resident may be to organize cover for and control British MI6 agents in that particular country.

The British MI6 also has deep cover agents. These deep cover agents more often than not don't allow flexibility of operations on the part of the agent involved. Usually, these agents rely on their stations for communication, guidance and administrative support. They often have covers as journalists. The difference between a British MI6 deep cover officer and a deep cover agent is that the deep cover officer is always employed by the British MI6 while the deep cover agent is always recruited to work as agents under a British MI6 officer and is paid to do so.

The British MI6 carries out covert operations. More often than not, some field agents are assigned to carry out these covert operations. Political actions are usually part of the covert operations and isn't limited to propaganda campaigns, creating secret radio and television stations, wrecking international conferences, organizing coups, assassinations and influencing elections. Covert operations having a part or whole of it with a military nature are not carried out by the British MI6 but by the Special Air Services (SAS) squadrons. It is clear that some sort of cooperation exists between the British MI6 and the SAS. The British

MI6 always briefs the SAS before and during any overseas operations.

The British MI6 uses private security firms and mercenaries to support governments favored by Her Majesty. The mercenaries are agents and more often times than not ex-SAS men and women looking for action abroad. The mercenaries are often used to provide training assistance to the regime supported by the British government. The military and security training assistance provided by the mercenaries are a form of covert operations. It provides opportunity for the British MI6 to gather intelligence about the country where the mercenaries are being employed.

The British MI6 liaises with the intelligence organizations of other nations of the world. The British MI6 may liaise with the CIA, the

Australian Secret Intelligence Services (ASIS), etc. The British MI6 exchanges clandestine reports; run defection programs; carries out joint political campaigns; joint surveillance operations with the intelligence organizations of the other nations of the world.

Analyzing the 1973 Chilean Coup That Ousted Salvador Allende – Chapter Nine

It is an open secret that the United States CIA was involved in the ousting of Salvador Allende, the Chilean president who got elected in the Chile of 1972. The complete history of this ordeal is everywhere on the internet and anyone who seeks to acquaint himself or herself with such a history, should look to the internet search engines for such knowledge. Allende was removed via a coup d'état because the West saw him as a threat to their economic interest. The aim of this chapter is not to teach history lessons on the ousting of Allende. Rather, the aim is to elucidate the points marshaled out in the previous chapters which clearly illustrates that Her Majesty's Government employs her predatory ideology when it comes to relating with the United States. We shall briefly analyze the 1973 Chilean coup in the light of these ideologies..

Parasitism; Predation:

The British MI6 as we know by now represents the eyes and brains of the British government. In a similar fashion, the CIA also represents the eyes and brains of the United States government. The Chilean coup of September 11, 1973 clearly shows the art of predation employed by the British government on the United States government. The coup d'état was paid for by the United States. Over 3 million US Dollars was spent on the execution of the coup. It was executed 95% by the United States intelligence agents. The United States

CIA was used as a secondary host to penetrate the Chilean government whom Her Majesty's Government eventually exploited by negotiating better copper import contracts with the Pinochet government (government of the man who took power after the ousting of Allende), thereby earning substantial foreign exchange through payments made in British pounds as well as selling military hardware and equipment to the Chilean government. By becoming a secondary host, the United States government only benefitted by having the ridiculous overcharges made by the Allende government overturned; as they tried to recoup losses made from nationalizing the copper industry in Chile.

Camouflage:
      The British government concealed the real reasons why they

wanted to remove Allende from the United States government. They only fronted economic interests as a reason for working with the United States government to depose of Salvador Allende. The real reason for using the United States CIA to orchestrate the coup d'état against Allende, was primarily to further the interests of the British Empire in Latin America and to do so without suspicion. Another primary aim for orchestrating the coup d'état was to weaken the United States government and eventually make her subservient (by default; due to the effects of predation) to Her Majesty's Government controls and manipulation. The economic interest reason was only a camouflage for the British government to exploit the United States government and consolidate her imperialism in Latin America. The camouflage techniques employed by the British was suitable to the United States government psyche if probed more. The United States government after the Second World War was in a psychological frame of mind that made it see every nation on earth as a potential threat to the United States. It's unfair to blame the United States for acting in such a manner because she has never imagined that the World War II would have such a devastating effect on the peace of her citizens and that the threats posed by Nazi Germany would threaten the continental United States as you know it. Therefore any imagined threat thrown at the United States at that period of time, would've been accepted as real and there would've been an urgent need to act on it. The sense of pride of the United States government was also manipulated to make her believe that she was saddled with the duty of enforcing world peace especially after she considered her contributions in defeating the Nazis and the consequent gains thereof.

Mimicry:

By mimicry, Her Majesty's government preyed upon the United States government and her people. This assertion is true; if you consider the fact that the British government "appeared" to share very common beliefs with the United States government such as the United States belief in democracy instead of communism; the belief in free market capitalism instead of socialism or Marxism and the United States belief in freedom instead of slavery. The British government since 1776 has always seen the United States as a part of her lost Empire and will always do whatever is humanly possible to regain her back. These mimicries were actually feigned in great contrast to the actual beliefs of Her Majesty's government. As you may know, the British government has a monarch; she also ran one of the most aggressive slave trade rackets ever in history; her government runs on a socialist economic system; her democracy is as good as communism, if at all it isn't communism. The real beliefs of Her Majesty's government are in reality in stark contrast to that of the United States government, but she still manages to mimic the United States dearly held values with the sole aim of weakening (by consequence of her predation) the suspicion as well as to control and manipulate the United States government and her resources (financial or otherwise). The United States government has indeed been weakened structurally to a very large extent by the prolonged wars the British MI6 continues to engineer and manipulate her to fight all over the world. These wars destroy the vitality

of the United States and her people.
Mimicry is one of the behavioral
mechanisms of polypus Britain that
encourages these wars.

Octopus; Polypus:
     The British government has been
compared to a polypus in chapter
four of this book. The polypus Britain
has her tentacles firmly sunk in Latin
Americas till date. The Allende
government happened to be one of
those prey (host) that tried to resist
the British imperialism but found that
once a tentacle has been sunk in, it
was difficult for a prey to stop a
predator from feeding on it. The
copper rich Chile held great
enticements for Her Majesty's
Government because she needed
copper for her industries in Britain.
An expanding empire would need
copper and other metallic minerals
necessary for the production of
certain consumer goods. The British

polypus tentacles are clearly seen in her exploitation of the copper resources in Chile through proxy companies controlled by Her Majesty's government. This continued up until the election of Allende who was hell bent on nationalizing the copper mining industry of Chile so that it would become state owned and in his view, the profits would benefit the people of Chile. The British government was not going to take this move that also in her view will make Britain lose substantial foreign exchange to the Chilean government. The coup d'état was planned solely by the British MI6 and her plan was to front the United States government for the execution of the overthrow as well as use the CIA and its resources to carry this out. The reader must not forget that during this period in history, the United States government was totally under the strict control and manipulations of the British government and this made her very vulnerable to any sort of suggestions from the British government. At this period in history, the British government dug in her tentacles deeply into the United States CIA, the brains and eyes of the United States government. Once the tentacles were sunk in, the United States CIA was became structurally adjusted to be the front for and fund projects that were to the advantages of the so called "sister" British MI6.

Empire:

The British Empire is always seeking to expand her territories. The British monarchy ensures that this line of thought and action is towed by the British government. The idea behind the imperialistic view of the world by Her Majesty's government clearly lies in her hubris and in her quest for the economic prosperity of the British people. For emphasis sake, Her Majesty's government considers the United States as a lost territory. By Jove, she seeks to reacquire this territory by hook or crook. The solemn oath to accomplish this was taken by the British government since 1776 and hasn't changed a bit if you have carefully followed the history of the relations between the United States and Britain. So far as the British government was concerned, the United States and her peoples were to remain under her Empire. The British monarchy won't change this particular view anytime soon. Hence, the prioritized need for Her Majesty's government to manipulate the United States and bring her under her total control. The thought of using the United States government and her resources to consolidate her gains in the Latin America's wasn't a bad idea to Her Majesty's government especially if you considered the fact that the United States as one of her wealthiest territories (thinking like the British Monarchy), will readily provide the front and resources for such consolidations. It was certainly a game of chess. The United States as a front for the British government allows Her Majesty's government to maintain her prestige and by providing the resources of such operations to be carried out successfully, the United States acted as a typical prey would act as well as fixed itself in such a way that denying involvement would prove fatal. Like any typical British mastermind, through the might of one of her territories (the secondary host), she would maintain control over another of her territories (primary host). The British government's control and manipulation ensured that the United States CIA at her call and beckoning will overthrow the government of any nation that threatened the economic interests of Her Majesty Empire. Like in every parasitic relationship, the United States became weaker while the British Empire grew stronger.

Divide and Rule:

The ousting of Salvador Allende as the head of the Chilean government was not planned by the United States CIA but by the British MI6; the reader must not forget this. The divide and rule tactics was always employed by the British government as a major tool of controlling the British Empire subjects. The Chilean Coup of 1973 presents a good case that argues in the favor of this assertion. The coup d'état was carried out from the standpoint that the United States government perceived that the Allende government was threatening the strategic economic interests of the

United States government. Her Majesty's government through the British MI6 controlled the United States CIA (which mirrored the British MI6) and manipulated her at that particular period in history and presented certain conclusions that favored the conspiracy of an Allende government hostility to United States strategic economic interests by passing on suggestions that supported such a narrative in the daily intelligence briefings presented to the United States president. The idea being that the United States Congress and the United States President will indeed see Allende from the British MI6 perspective. The divide and rule tactics was craftily employed in dividing the then United States government from the Allende government on the basis of the strategic economic interests of the United States government being threatened by the nationalization of copper mining industries in Chile by the Allende's government and the so perceived leanings towards the "communist bloc".. The United States CIA believed her British MI6 partners without first verifying if truly the Allende's government was hostile to United States strategic economic interests. This recklessness on the part of the United States CIA ensured that she was being manipulated into doing the bidding of Her Majesty's government. You must understand that at this point in history, the United States CIA was receiving and giving valuable information to the British MI6. This intelligence sharing gave room for the complete dictation of the United States foreign policy by the British government. The United States CIA was certainly not wise to these manipulations and certainly didn't see British machinations in the Allende affair. The divide and rule tactics was also employed in the ousting of Allende. The Allende government was totally divided at the time of the coup d'état. The military junta led by Pinochet was in discordant tune with the Chilean congress that wanted the continuity of Salvador Allende and did vote for the nationalization of the State's copper mining industry. The British government through the United States CIA preyed on this visible division and succeeded in ousting Allende who had quite a number of enemies in the Chilean military.

Corruption:
Prior to the end of the Second World War, the British MI6 continued its policy of sharing intelligence with the United States Office of Strategic Services (the OSS) as they battled together Nazi Germany during that time. Another stuff the United States OSS and British MI6 did together

during war time was the "covert action' stuff. The covert action stuff was the purely illegal activities that took place during the war like economic sabotage, assassination, black propaganda, etc. The examples of these covert actions engaged in during war times varied in accordance to the situation in which it was needed to be employed at that time. The British MI6 understood this, but not the OSS that was very young and inexperienced at that point in time. The "corruption by covert action" ensued after the United States CIA was given the mandate to carry out these "covert actions" across the globe and it ensured that the United States foreign policy took a liking to solving global political problems with the idea of doing anything that was illegally within her powers to have her way with the various countries that the United States felt threatened its strategic economic interests (Would it be wrong to write British economic interests?) as well as the world "peace". The "corruption by covert action" enabled corruption to eat very deep into the fabrics of the United States government especially when you considered that it was being employed by the United States government during peace times. Ideally created for war times, "covert action" by its nature wasn't supposed to be used to destabilize the governments of other nations during peace times rather diplomacy with a tinge of understanding ought to have taken precedence in creating a harmonious world and if it fails then sanctions by the international community follow suit. The corruption that covert action brought along with it made the United States a sucker for wars. As corruption does, it poisoned the United States democracy, divided the United States Congress and took the mind of the various Presidents of the United States after the Second World War away from the betterment of the United States people. The people suffered. The corruption of government makes government do things in secret. The United States government was no exception to this fact especially after the Second World War; this was exactly what the British Empire wanted. The divisions created by the poison of corruption through covert actions had increasingly created an American society that found it okay to invade Korea, Vietnam, Kuwait, Afghanistan, Iraq, Syria, Yemen and many other societies invaded through the might of the United States and under the strict control and manipulation of the United States government by Her Majesty's government. The Chilean affair showed firsthand what the poison of corruption (illegality) can do to a morally upright society. The creation of an American society where good was compromised for evil was the desire of the British government towards the United States and as the reader will understand, a divided and corrupt society can easily be controlled and manipulated.

Analyzing the 1964 Brazilian Coup that Ousted Joao Goulart – Chapter Ten

This chapter shall be as self explanatory as Chapter Nine; the reason being that whatsoever shall be written in this chapter shall consolidate the gains of Chapter Nine. The first thing you need to understand about the whole affair was that the United States government had no idea why the Goulart administration appeared to have stronger leanings to "communism and socialism". According to the assessment of the United States government, these leanings threatened her strategic economic interests. Let's pause for a second and reflect on what might have caused the United States government to buy into the idea of the Goulart government having socialist and communist inclinations. Is it very possible that the Goulart administration was painted to appear "communist" and at the same time the real reason (behind the ousting of Joao Goulart on March 31st, 1964) for doing so was then carefully hidden by the British government so that the United States and her resources will be used to further expand Her Majesty's Empire without suspecting any foul play? This chapter shall seek to understudy the Goulart travails based on the parameters used to analyze the Allende affair.

Predation; Parasitism:
     The British MI6 through the United States CIA (a secondary host), sunk her tentacles into the Brazilian government led by Goulart to ensure

that the British Empire continued its expansion at the detriment of the Brazilian people. You must understand that after the Second World War (shall I say after defeating the Nazis), the British foreign policy took another turn. The turn was to use the United States to destroy Soviet Empire and influence; consolidate British control and manipulation in the Latin Americas; consolidate British control and manipulation in the Middle East (the focus now on Iran today); consolidate British control and manipulation in Asia (the focus now on North Korea today); and finally consolidate her manipulations and controls in what will now be the very weakened and divided United States. The need for Her Majesty's government to consolidate her gains in Africa, wasn't as profound as her cogent needs in the Eastern Europe and the Latin Americas (especially during the so called "Cold War" era) because the colonization of Africa allowed her to establish a strong presence and influence in the Africa; the reader can perceive this clearly. The plot of the British government was to use the United States government through the CIA to carry out these global domination escapades that will eventually ensure that Her Majesty's government controlled the entire globe. The United States when considered in the light of predation cum parasitism can be seen as a very perfect secondary host. She unwittingly and unconsciously feeds the British Empire expansionism and therefore loses her own vitality in the process. Remember that in every parasitic relationship, the host never wins. The host always dies whether it is the secondary or the primary host.

Camouflage:

It is certainly clear that by now, the reader understands that Her Majesty's government employs camouflage when it comes to dealing with the nations she considers as preys. The camouflage allows her to carefully conceal her intentions while at the same time projecting a form which the prey nation wouldn't suspect a bit. The art of camouflaging in the present world requires careful attention to details. The British government must be credited for mastering this art that has made her control nations of which the United States government is no exception. The Goulart ousting takes us into the familiar territories of sheer British camouflage in the globe. The main reasons for initiating in the Goulart affair was carefully hidden and a pretext presented instead which made it "appear" like the Goulart administration was threatening the strategic economic interests of the United States government. The United States government never understood that the whole idea for British government wanting the ousting of the so called "communist" leaders in the Latin Americas was done to pave way for the expansion of Her Majesty's Empire and the consolidation of her imperialistic powers in that region. The "economic interests" pointed at by the British government were only decoys and a careful way to conceal the fact that the British government was using the United States government to further her interests. It was the ultimate manipulation.

Mimicry:

The British government employed mimicry once again in her dealings with the United States government as she consolidated her gains in the Latin Americas. The

British government appeared to have shared similar value systems with the United States government especially in the areas of the United States government fight against communism, socialism and slavery. These so called areas of common interests if you remember clearly were areas the United States CIA trusted the British MI6 to work together on. Unfortunately, the British government had her own agenda, quite different from that of the United States. The fight against communism, socialism, slavery was "the bait" for the United States by Her Majesty's government; a bait which the United States government swallowed hook, line and sinker. The Goulart coup d'état clearly shows the ingenuity of Her Majesty's government in the aspect of perfectly utilizing mimicry. The British government appeared to have been fighting communism, socialism and slavery alongside their "allies" the United States, meanwhile they had an ulterior motive for doing so. Their motive was to consolidate their gains in the Latin Americas as well strengthen Her Majesty's influence and grip on the states that mattered to Her Majesty's government in the region. The reader by now must be very conversant on how the British value systems differs from the United States value systems especially when it comes to freedom, democracy, and capitalism. Is it not clear to the reader's perception that Her Majesty's government employed this natural behavioral mechanism to control and manipulate the United States government and in the process weaken her?

Octopus; Polypus

An important question the reader must ask himself or herself at this point is; why Brazil? As you must notice, Brazil is in the Latin Americas, a region of the world where oil and gas is in abundance. One of the aims of an empire is to ensure that it controls the resources of all her territories. Therefore, anything acting as an opposition to that control will be removed by any means possible. The Goulart government's control of the profits and foreign exchange leaving Brazil at that particular period in time meant that she threatened the British government (predator) desire of feeding on the resources of Brazil and her people (prey). The tentacle of the British government in the Latin Americas covers the entire Latin America region today. Like the Romans at the height of their glory, no nation of the earth was to be left out of the control of Her Majesty's Empire; the basic aim of the British government was to conquer, control and manipulate these other nations.

The British government needed to consolidate these gains in the Latin Americas just like she did in Africa during the colonial times. The truth remains that Her Majesty's government gained a lot of imperialistic experiences in Africa during the colonial times; an experience which the United States was never opportune to gain. The United States vulnerability in this key area (that is the area of imperialism) made her very naive in her dealing with British cunning and wit. You must understand that the British monarchy has overtime dealt with the tricks and machinations of the various kingdoms that existed in Europe during the medieval times; and this was the type of experience the United States government never had. This inexperience made the United States government very vulnerable and naive when it came to handling of her international affairs.

The United States failed to understand that Old kingdoms of Europe were always scheming and plotting to bring down other kingdoms in their vain glory. This type of game is a "game of supremacy". A game in which there are no rules. A game of man eats man and dog eats dog. It's a cold world out there and the United States government was definitely left out in the cold. The British government has shown themselves masters of the "game of supremacy" and that's why they've got their tentacles spreading out like wildfire all over the world especially with the unwitting help of the United States and her resources which was being controlled and manipulated by Her Majesty's government to achieve this purpose,

Empire:

Her Majesty's government understands that it is practically impossible for any nation to build an empire without having those whom they controlled, manipulated and exploited. The failure of other nations of the world to understand this, was indeed to their great detriment. The reader must also appreciate by now that the inability to understand these simple principle, will lead to the ruin of empires. It's the classic game of throne; the throne in this case to be deemed as the supremacy over the world. The United States and her people see itself as only but a great country on earth; this is clearly in contrast to the way the British government sees her. Her Majesty's government sees her as her subject and itself as an Empire; an empire that's always expanding at that; an empire to be ruled with subtlety and wit, in great contrast to the Roman

Empire that was ruled majorly by brute force. The Goulart affair allows us to examine Her Majesty's Empire from the viewpoint of her maintaining a strong grip on Latin Americas and aligning any of the states that made up the region back to order if they deviated from the wishes of the Empire. The facts elucidated so far requires careful meditation upon. As a matter of fact, any state or territory in the world that threatened the interest of Her Majesty's Empire shall quickly be aligned to order. The alignment of the Goulart administration by Her Majesty's government exemplifies this fact. The ever expanding British Empire is always looking for a willing tool that will be employed in the furtherance of her objectives. The United States government presented itself as a willing tool for that purpose through her recklessness or shall I say, was chosen by Her

Majesty's Empire to aid in the consolidation of her gains and the maintenance of the iron grip of Her Majesty's Empire on the Brazilian people. The failure of the Goulart government to understand this led to her quick demise; and the inability of the United States government to understand that she was being a willing tool that was being used in the furtherance of the British Empire's interests has greatly weakened her governmental structure and ensured that British government's presence and influence in the United States is strong. The United States and her people are ignorant to this fact that's why for over seventy years she has been controlled and manipulated by Her Majesty's Empire whims and caprices.

Divide and Rule:

No nation on earth has mastered the art of divide and rule like the Britain. The truth remains that Britain has exploited this tactics in the furtherance of her objective of dominating the entire world. The key questions to be asked in the very sordid Goulart affair is this: Was the United States CIA manipulated into believing that the Goulart regime posed a serious threat to the United States strategic economic interests? This key question is no small question at all. It throws great light on the divide and rule tactics employed by the British government when dealing with other nations of the world, this time a very bright one. If the author were to answer that question, he will answer 'yes', Her Majesty's government actually manipulated the United States government into orchestrating the coup d'état that ousted Joao Goulart and installed Castelo Branco. The reasons that support a British manipulation of the United States CIA are very obvious. The first amongst it being that the British government needed to align one of her subjects whom she believed was rebelling against her Empire. Secondly, from an ideological viewpoint, a parasitic predator can use a prey (the secondary host) to control and feed on another prey (the primary host). Remember, that Her Majesty's government always considered the United States to be one of her territories. There was no other way to achieve the aligning of the Brazilian government where British oil and gas interests were threatened except to make the United States believe that her "strategic interests" were being threatened as well as manipulating her into aligning the Goulart administration. The United States fell for the ploy. The Goulart government was also divided using the medieval divide and rule tactics. In the course of the coup d'état the British government had advised the United States to create factions in the Brazilian military and congress. The factions created were divided into those who were for Goulart (a minority) and those who were against Goulart (a majority). At the end of the coup d'état, the military finally succeeded in ousting a democratically elected Joao Goulart as president. The result was another huge gain for Her Majesty's Empire and a great loss for the United States and the Brazil.

Corruption:
     Nothing destroys a nation faster than corruption. The British government understood the preceding

statement very clearly and applied it thoroughly in her dealings with the other nations of the world. The truth remains is to, corrupt all the peoples that make up a nation is very difficult but to corrupt those that govern a nation is as easy as ABC and it simply entails destroying the moral compass of those who govern the nation. It's easier to corrupt an individual when the basic instincts that ensure the survival of the individual have been threatened. Whenever an individual or an organism has its survival threatened, it easily falls into the hands of a master manipulator. The greatest time to apply the art of corruption in government (that is to corrupt the individuals in government) is when certain factions of that government feel threatened by the actions of the other factions. When you've thoroughly divided the government of that nation based on ideologies;

then it becomes a walk over to corrupt the individuals in that government. The British government perfectly understands the above facts as pertains to corruption. Absolute power corrupts absolutely. This maxim holds sway in all spheres of life. The individuals that make up a government usually find it difficult to relinquish their powers due to benefits that come with the positions of power. The British government also understands this. There's no other way to portray the corruption of the United States government by Her Majesty's government except through understanding that her activities after the Second World War (Can I say after the British-German War?) were totally illegal. Remember, that the aim of corruption is to make the individual do illegal things or commit vices. When corruption comes into the life of an individual or organization or nation, it eats deep into their moral fabrics. It makes them think vice as okay. It undermines the moral uprightness or the righteousness of the individual or organization or nation. When this happens, equality is destroyed and justice erased. The society decays from inside out just like Ancient Rome and Egypt decayed from inside out. The society collapses and the people suffer miserably. The United States government today is on the verge of decay, no thanks to the poison of "covert action" by the British government. The poison injected into the United States government right after World War II; a poison that has slowly been killing the American Republic; a poison that subjected the United States to the worst of manipulations; a poison that has made the United States visit other nations of the world with mayhem and catastrophe; a poison that has decayed the United States justice system; a poison that has made the United States leave the path of truth and justice to the path of lies and injustice. The very nature of "covert action' entails lies and injustice. Any action that employs assassination, black propaganda, and economic sabotage is truly based on lies and injustice. The United States deviated and became an object of manipulation and control by her enemies. Corruption was definitely employed indirectly in the toppling of the Goulart government. As directed by the British MI6, the United States CIA bribed military officers in the then Goulart government as well as members of the Brazilian congress to ensure that Joao Goulart was replaced by Castelo Branco who inadvertently danced to the tunes of the British Empire. Immediately Goulart was toppled, Her Majesty's Empire followed through with the sales of arms to the Brazilian government, thus consolidating the gains of the coup d'état. These arms also ensured that the new government remained unthreatened by any element within Brazil. Such powers in the hands of Branco corrupted the Brazilian government further; an exact situation wanted by Her Majesty's government because once again, "absolute power always corrupts absolutely". I want the reader to always remember this maxim.

Analysis of the 1964 South Vietnam Coup That Ousted Ngo Dinh Diem – Chapter Eleven

The South Vietnam coup of 1964 was orchestrated to overthrow Ngo Dinh Diem and install Durong Van Minh. The coup d'état took place on November 1, 1964 and led to the assassination of the president of the First Republic of South Vietnam. The United States government involvement in the coup was no secret, but what was kept a secret was the British government involvement in the overthrow. The details of the Ngo Dinh Diem coup d'état is out there in the annals of history for anyone who wants to look them up to do so. This chapter like the previous chapters seeks to examine in a similar light the 1964 South Vietnam coup d'état that led to the overthrow of the Ngo Dinh Diem administration; using all the criteria that depicts the predatory nature of Her Majesty's government:

Predation; Parasitism:

By now, the reader must have thoroughly understood that predators always live off the vitality of their prey (hosts). A predator is very keen on surviving, that's why it looks for preys. The Diem affair sheds good light on why the British government predatory instincts have led to her feeding on the United States government. The parasitic relationship existing between Her Majesty's government and the United States government is clearly seen in the Ngo Dinh Minh ousting. The British government once again used the United States government as a secondary host to firmly dig its tentacles into the South Vietnamese government a primary host; the aim being to feed on the appetizing resources of the South Vietnamese territories which includes bauxite, copper, oil and gas as well as other mineral resources Her Majesty's Empire deems fit to be beneficiary to her expansion. The British government penetrated the United States (secondary host) through the Office of Strategic Services (OSS) (now the CIA); through the CIA, she sunk her tentacles deep into the live wire of the United States government and the sapping began. The Diem overthrow was carried out by the United States government with the encouragement and support of the British government. The result was the same as a parasite causing the secondary host to make structural adjustments that will enable it feed through the secondary host. The

United States government like any secondary host will behave, provided the resources (funds) for Durong Van Minh and his generals to execute the coup that ousted the South Vietnamese president. As always the United States lost while the British government gained. The end results was eventually the further expansion of Her Majesty's Empire and the consolidation of her gains in Asia.

Camouflage:

The United States government dealt with the British government with very open and trusting hands after the Second World War. That made the United States government very vulnerable especially if you considered the fact that Her Majesty's government never dealt with the United States in the same capacity. The British government cleverly hid their own motives for encouraging the South Vietnamese coup of 1964.

The United States never saw the big picture. The British government artfully concealed the big picture from the United States government. The British government remained hidden throughout the South Vietnamese affair of 1964. The British government was basically invisible during the whole affair, providing only planning and advisory support to the United States during the ordeal. Her Majesty's government as at that period in history didn't allow the visibility of the British MI6 in the Ngo Dinh Diem coup of 1964. The United States and her CIA on the other hand were very visible during the coup, taking center stage and having the whole stage lights beamed on them; and again taking the fall for Her Majesty's government; which meant that Her Majesty's government preserved her prestige while the United State government was labeled the "imperialists".

At this point, the reader must understand that the United States government since its formation never sought to be an imperialist nation (the author states this with all conviction because he properly understands the United States history pre-World War II). The British government tactfully and subtly made the United States government a sucker for her whims and caprices. The plans made and strategies formulated by Her Majesty's government turned the United States into the true definition of an "imperialist". The United States government, who was a true defender of global freedom and justice now became an usurper of liberty and rule of law through the control and manipulation of the British government who continues to hide in the shadows; she carefully hides while the United States makes herself very loud and obvious, thus making lots of enemies in the process. Some of the South Vietnamese men and women who were friends with Ngo Dinh Diem declared the United States government as imperialist right after his death. Her Majesty's government was never mentioned at all in that light.

Mimicry:

The analysis of the previous coup d'états that involved Allende and Goulart were analyzed from a different viewpoint of mimicry and was purely restricted in its analysis to the fact that the British government had appeared to share similar value systems with the United States government. In this particular chapter the coup that ousted Diem shall be analyzed from the "alliance" perspective. The "alliance" perspective allows the reader to understand how by sleight of wit and the illusion of events, the British government was able to appear to the United States as an ally. The "alliance" trick is an old Machiavellian one used by the various kingdoms in Europe to penetrate their allies. Old Medieval Europe was very aware of these tricks but the United States which was a very new republic unfortunately wasn't well informed as to the manner of machinations of these old kingdoms. After the Second World War, the British MI6 undertook the task of nurturing the then Office of Strategic Services (OSS) of the United States. This act of nurturing the seemingly burgeoning new intelligence service of the United States (now the CIA) allowed the British MI6 to ingrain itself as the trusted ally of the United States government. A very clever move if you look at it. Immediately the British government had done this, it was easy to build other new alliances that appeared to the United States to be very genuine. As the reader is expected to deduce, any alliance that the United States government has forged with the guidance of the British government is tainted with control and manipulation. No matter how innocuous such an alliance appears to be, it is an alliance that will certainly always benefit Her Majesty's Empire and at the same time weaken the United States government. The Diem affair was very rife with this Britain and United States alliance. The British MI6 had planned the coup right from day one; they only needed to sell it to the United States government in a way that will stir them into action on behalf of Her Majesty's Empire. The United States was made to believe that the Ngo Dinh Diem's government was persecuting Buddhists in South Vietnam. The

United States government was also made to believe that the Diem administration was carrying out land reforms that led to a disadvantaged relocation of peasant farmers in a way that didn't favor the local populace. The United States government was typically manipulated into believing that Ngo Dinh Diem was no longer serving the Western interests anymore. The beliefs made the United States government take the ousting of Diem very personal; thus, the British MI6 plan given to the United States CIA was used to oust Diem. The ousting created a fertile ground for Her Majesty's government to take the spoils of the coup d'état. As always, Her Majesty's prestige and influence grew while the infamy of the United States in Asia also grew alongside it.

Octopus; Polypus:

The British government has continued its policy of spreading and sinking her tentacles into the different nations across the globe that vitalizes the economy of Her Majesty. The United States can't nurture imperialistic ambitions like the British government because the United States by default wasn't created to be a Empire. For emphasis sake, I repeat, the United States wasn't created by her founders to become an Empire; rather it was created to be a republic that upheld the values of freedom and justice. Any move by the United States to become anything but a republic will definitely be a catastrophe because she will be going against her very nature. Her Majesty's government nevertheless was setup to be an Empire. And by nature, an Empire will always seek expansion; seek to dominate and control her territories;

seek to exploit her subjects and make them subservient to the head of the Empire. An Empire can never be a Republic; but a Republic can become an Empire. A Republic doesn't recognize a monarch rather it recognizes a Senate but an Empire will always recognize a monarch. The monarch is the figure head of an Empire while the president is the figure head of a Republic. The reader must understand the key difference between the duos (that is a Republic and an Empire). The Polypus has multiple tentacles like the Empire has multiple territories it controls. The Diem overthrow was planned by Her Majesty's government to ensure that she had access to the plum mineral resources of the South Vietnamese territories as well as to consolidate her gains in Asia. Like an octopus digs a tentacle through its sucker appendages into a prey, so did the British government through the

United States CIA exploit the South Vietnamese resources. It is common knowledge by now that the United States resources (funds) were used to sponsor the coup d'état that led to the assassination of Ngo Dinh Diem. The United States in doing so helped Her Majesty's government in aligning to its whims and caprices an administration she felt wasn't structurally adjusted to allow it exploit the territories of the South Vietnamese people. The concomitant effect was the quick structural adjustment of the South Vietnamese government to the wishes of the British government through the United States government. The same way a host (prey) would structurally adjust to meet the needs of a parasite (predator).

Empire:

The ousting of Ngo Dinh Diem by the United States government was carried out in the favor of the British government. Her Majesty's government is very careful when it comes to the various dealings she has with her subjects. The dealings of Her Majesty's government with the nations that make up her Empire is very calculated. Like a chess player, the British government thinks through every move that she makes on the chessboard. She ponders through it over and over again before making the decisive move. Therefore, it comes as no surprise that the British government was able to manipulate and control the United States government to help her consolidate her gains in the world. The British government understands that every strategic move on the chessboard draws the player towards victory (checkmate). The United

States government has not thought of such a game, simply because she has no imperialistic ambitions. However, the case is very different for the British government that sees the world from a different perspective. Her Majesty's government sees the world as a place for the British man or woman to dominate. Her Majesty's government sees itself as the one to promulgate this domination. As always, there can be no domination without manipulation and control. The quest to cater for the prosperity of British people is secondary to the British government's aim to dominate the governments of other nations. One can argue that such domination will bring prosperity to any nation that thinks from an imperialistic point of view, but one needs to be careful not to forget the pillages and damages that result from this quest to dominate. If the reader carefully contrasts the ideologies of domination with equality which both guides the policies (by default) of both the British government and the United States government respectively, you may safely conclude that British government ideology promotes "the prosperity of Her Majesty's government through domination and exploitation" whereas the United States government ideology promotes "the prosperity of the United States through freedom and commerce". It's very obvious from what we've discussed that the ideology of Her Majesty's government runs in sharp contrast to those of the United States government in all spheres of life. What this means is that the British government's foreign policies are very different from her domestic policies. The British government's foreign policies can be seen from the viewpoint of ideology as "total domination, control, manipulation and exploitation" of the globe and that of the United States as "democracy, diplomacy and commerce". Whatever is the case, it is very important that the reader understands what has been written so far. One can argue that the territories of both Britain and the United States determine to a large extent the nature of the kind of government that they can pursue. If this is the case, is it possible to say that Britain being without much needed mineral resources should forage on other nations through control and manipulations (that is domination and exploitation from an imperialistic viewpoint)? Is it also possible to assume that the United States being of a larger territory with infinite mineral resources is best fitted to trade with other nations? What if other nations in the world acted in the same manner as Her Majesty's government, what would be the resultant effect? If the United States dropped its free commerce policies and foraged on other nations, does it guarantee her ultimate natural selection? What makes it a natural selection if it's being manipulated? Is it possible to beat nature at its own game? If we obeyed nature's laws, aren't we best fitted to survive better? Wasn't it what the United States framers observed? The truth remains that the British government thrives to expand her Empire at the expense of the rest of the world.

Divide and Rule:

In this chapter, it will please the author to analyze the divide and rule tactics employed by the British government in the control and manipulations of other nations they deal with. The British government carries out her typical divide and rule tactics using British agents working in the governments which they aim to control and manipulate. The British agent (in this case a policy adviser) is sent to work for or become acquainted with high level ranking officials (or anyone close to the high ranking official) in the government they wish to malign. Once a relationship exists between the British agent and the government official or anyone Her Majesty's government believes will influence the said government official, the British government asks the agent to make demands which they believe will inadvertently make the said government official or anyone who could influence him to act in a manner that yields the desired results. The prominent feature of the British "divide and rule" tactics which we have not mentioned so far is that it is very "indirect" in nature. The lack of direct contact between a British MI6 official and an agent makes it difficult to trace any maligning back to Her Majesty's government. It is certainly a very vital characteristic of the British government. The art of indirectly influencing individuals to work in the favor of Her Majesty's government is one which the British MI6 has mastered. It's like telepathy (your ability to control someone's thought process ensures that they do whatever you want them to do). It flows in a chain series of causes and effects, of which for every effect produced, there is a certain cause. The results are devastating because you never get to see the hands that caused the events. Magical, isn't? The British MI6 artfully employed this divide and rule technique in manipulating the United States CIA into believing that Diem wasn't the right man anymore. It was a matter of simply making the United States believe that Diem was persecuting the Buddhists by planting false stories in the Daily Nationals of the

South Vietnamese papers to corroborate whatever intelligence they had to pass on to the United States government. As always, the United States swallowed the sham hook line and sinker. The United States CIA didn't bother to verify the information passed on to her but she rather chose to believe whatever intelligence that was passed on by the British MI6. This is a very terrible mistake to make in intelligence gathering. It is always important to investigate any source of information. It is foolish to believe any information that you are given. "Not to believe any information given to you" is certainly one piece of advice the British MI6 never gave the United States CIA. They knew that hinting the United States government on anything of that sort meant the discovery and the total ruination of the plans of the expansion of Her Majesty's Empire.

Corruption:

It's no small matter when a state becomes poisoned with corruption. It quickly leads to the ruination of the state if the poison isn't neutralized. Corruption is fast destroying nations under the British government hegemony; the reason being that Her Majesty's government can only exploit a nation when its moral foundation is very weak. The weaker the moral foundation of a nation, the easier it is for the British government to exploit. The poison of corruption is injected into any social system to weaken and exploit it. Corruption make take many forms but whatever form it takes, it basically involves one structure and that structure is disregard for the rule of law (lawlessness). Wherever corruption thrives, some group of persons always tend to make their own rules which they believe isn't applicable to others. Corruption thrives in a society where inequality thrives. Where one sect of people are made to feel that they are above the law and the others must obey their laws. Corruption is the bane of any society. From a global perspective, corruption make take the form of some nations of the world becoming outlaws (that is not subject to international laws and norms) and coercing other nations of the world to act according to their whims and caprices. The reader must understand that any nation that acts in a corrupt manner is by default, bound to have her domestic government corrupted over time. For Her Majesty's government, there would've been no other way to corrupt the United States except through making the United States disobey the international laws. Her Majesty's government understands that once the sense of lawlessness creeps in, it becomes difficult to remove such a way of life from the society. The British government then sought for a way to accomplish the seemingly impossible feat of corrupting the United States and the only way to do it was to inject the poison of "foreign policy by covert action". The reader must understand that the "very nature of any foreign policy by covert action" makes it very impossible for diplomacy to thrive in any nation which adopts it. What the ideology of "foreign policy by covert action" (totally aghast to the United States framers ideas of foreign policy by commerce and diplomacy) did was to make the United States government act in a rogue manner when dealing with other nations of the world". The idea of lawlessness crept in slowly but assuredly. The United States Congress members bought into this idea of having their way in the world through "covert action" which basically means not dealing fairly with (cheating) other nations of the world. The United States government blindly bought into the idea of "foreign policy by covert action" and as a result championed the assassinations of the presidents of other nations, the sabotage of the economies of other nations, the malicious manipulations of the thoughts of the people of other nations and all the rogue stuff you do in war times. The truth is that the United States government was manipulatively cajoled by the British government into behaving like she was at war with the world. And truly for the United States, she was always at war with the world. The hypersensitivity of the United States almost became her undoing because under that hypersensitivity, she bought the idea she was always faced with constant threats that needed to be confronted only through "covert action" and not diplomacy. The reader must also understand that if you've members of United States Congress who've been slowly but effectively buying into the ideas of doing things illegally in the international community, then there's no way they won't buy into the idea of doing things illegally in their domestic community (the United States Homeland}. So, the reader may observe that the author is trying to say that it's difficult to act in a rogue manner at the foreign level without doing the same at the domestic level. Corruption acts as a catalyst for the ruination of Republics; no exceptions. The Diem affair proves what the author has written so far right. Diem was overthrown because the United States government was a sucker for "foreign policy by covert action". As a sucker for "covert action", the right move to make by the United States government was to approve the assassination of Diem (a very illegal thing to do). The solution to all the United States international problems was the illegal natured "covert action". This alone made the United States government officials privy to or engaging in the "covert actions" criminals. It was also easy for the United States government through her agents in South Vietnam to corrupt Darung Van Minh. The British MI6 had been understudying Minh and understood that he was the jealous and vengeful type. They understood that Minh was the type to be easily corrupted. This weakness of Minh made him do exactly what the United States CIA (also doing the bidding of the British MI6) wanted him to do. It was only a question of paying Minh to do the dirty work. The reader can also observe that corruption works in a chain series (that is Mr. A corrupts Mr. B; Mr. B corrupts Mr. C; Mr. C corrupts Mr. D; Mr. D corrupts Mr. E, it goes on and on to infinity).

Analysis of the 1960 Democratic Republic of Congo Coup that Ousted Patrice Lumumba – Chapter Twelve

Our business as always is not to relate history but to accurately analyze without bias the various coup d'état that the United States government had participated in the past because of the British government's control and manipulation. The Patrice Lumumba saga analysis won't be different from what we've said so far in Chapters Nine, Ten and Eleven which analyzed the Allende, Goulart and Diem affairs respectively. Patrice Lumumba, the first Prime Minister of the

Democratic Republic of Congo was ousted from power on September 2, 1960 by Joseph Kasa-Vubu and Mobutu Sese Seko with the clandestine support of the United States government and the Belgian government. As always the two

governments that were directly involved in the coup d'état did so under the control and manipulations of Her Majesty's government. This chapter is very unique because the British government (the predator) preyed on the Democratic Republic of Congo using two secondary hosts. This chapter shall invariably use the same set of criteria employed in our analysis so far.

Predation; Parasitism
 The case of the ousting of Patrice Lumumba is special because for the first time in the book, the reader gets

to understand how Her Majesty's government was able to prey on the primary host using two secondary hosts. The secondary hosts in this case were the United States government and the Belgian government while the primary host was the Congolese government and her resources. The resources of the Democratic Republic of Congo includes but isn't limited to copper, oil, gold, diamond, bauxite and other mineral resources the British government seeks to exploit of the other nations of the world. The first thing the reader must observe in the Lumumba affair is that the resources of the Democratic Republic of Congo were also too alluring for any Empire to resist. Her Majesty's government had to have access to these resources in the territories of the Democratic Republic of Congo and Patrice Lumumba's nationalistic fervor was presenting an obstacle to achieving that purpose. The United States government before this affair had been greatly structurally adjusted (like any parasite would do to its host) to fight and destroy anything it felt had an appearance of "communism or socialism". The opposition to "communism or socialism" wasn't wrong but the approach to tackling it was in itself very wrong. The United States CIA was made to believe that Patrice Lumumba had communist leanings; and that was all they needed to believe; the United States CIA came after him with all they had. The British government once again sunk her tentacles into the United States government and the Belgian government and made them respond accordingly to her desires on the Democratic Republic of Congo. The United States being the Queen's knight always responded positively to anything Her Majesty's government gave it because she had been conditioned to do so right after the Second World War. The Belgian government also believed that Lumumba was the brain behind the massacre of white Belgians in the then Katanga Province. They also failed to verify the information given to them by the British MI6. As secondary hosts, both the United States government and the Belgian government were weakened structurally. They both lost vitality; the United States government spent up to $100,000 of her monies in the coup d'état whereas the Belgian government also lost her prestige and honor in the Democratic Republic of Congo after Lumumba's overthrow. The both suffered the loss of vital resources while Her Majesty's government grew in strength and honor.

Camouflage:

It's on record that the British government wanted Patrice Lumumba removed as soon as possible, because he was a hindrance to the expansion of their Empire. The reasons are very clear for all to see; Patrice Lumumba was a nationalist whose political ideologies and rhetoric made it very difficult for Her Majesty's government to consolidate her gains in Africa. Despite the British government's desires to oust Lumumba, they were never actually present in the whole affair that removed him. They were the mastermind of the angst against Lumumba, but they were never there to execute the plan. They cleverly hid. As always, the United States government was taking the center stage in the whole show and the Belgian government not as much as the United States government was but as well. The United States CIA wanted Lumumba out of the office of the prime minister. They even went to the extent of manufacturing a poisoned handkerchief in order to achieve this aim. The reasons presented to the United States government by the British government for the removal of Lumumba was that he had committed genocide and was a "communist". Her Majesty's government hid the fact that she was trying to expand her territories and her Empire as well. If only the United States government, a defender of global freedom, had known that there was an ulterior motive to this fact, she would have acted otherwise. The United States CIA also didn't know that she was being fixed by the British MI6 when the British MI6 passed on intelligence to her confirming that Patrice Lumumba was a communist. It's very clear to the reader at this point that "fighting communism or socialism" was the United States Achilles heel during this period in history; it was also the British government's hook while the need to further "freedom, democracy and capitalism" was the bait. All these facts were carefully hidden from the United States government (the prey) by Her Majesty's government (the predator).

Mimicry:

We had earlier mentioned that one of the tricks of the old kingdoms of the Medieval Europe was to spy on a strong enemy by allying with him. The process of appearing to ally with him makes him let down his guards, it allows you to study his strengths and weaknesses and when his strengths and weaknesses are understood, to use him as thou please. It is an old trick but a very effective one. It also allowed for the stealth infiltration of the enemies. Two of the oldest maxims in the world which the United States government failed to apply in her dealings with the world is "Man know thyself" and "Keep your friends close but your enemies closer". An enemy doesn't change its colors just like a leopard will never lose its spots. The gravest mistake made by the United States government was not to know itself. There's no person or organization in the universe which knows itself that'll be cajoled into trusting elements foreign to it. It's just impossible for such a thing to happen. Appearances are always feigned and that's why a man or woman who knows himself or herself isn't moved by it. Another mistake made by the United States government (of course which the

British government never did) was to think or believe that the British government had suddenly turned friends. One of the first laws that you're taught in Medieval Europe was never take an old enemy into confidence. Unfortunately, those who were in the corridors of power of the United States government immediately after the Second World War weren't privy to this knowledge. They took an old enemy into confidence. They also fell for simple appearances. The end result of disobeying this basic ancient political rule was the total ruination of a kingdom or Republic. The United States government as at the end of the war disobeyed certain laws which governed the interactions between Kingdoms and Republics. The author believes that the framers were well aware of these laws and were confident that the United States government will restrict her foreign dealings to only commerce and nothing else but commerce like they expected her to do. The Lumumba affair shows clearly that alliances can be very misleading. Her Majesty's government in her wits had created alliances that are structured to her own benefits and those of her people. Obviously these alliances don't favor the United States government. Permanent alliances like NATO, UN and many other alliances the United States government finds itself entangled in are to her very detriment and were very unwise decisions as such. The British government appeared to be an ally who fought communism and socialism alongside her comrade (the United States government) , but we know how false that appearance was. We understand how untrue the so called "alliance" between the United States government and the British government was. Patrice Lumumba was assassinated by firing squad on the basis of this alliance and the Belgian government was there to supervise the assassination. Was King Leopold II wise to these machinations? I don't think so.

Octopus; Polypus:

A polypus was defined in Chapter four as having multiple arms that were capable of being extended. Her Majesty's government can be defined in a similar fashion especially if you considered the definition of a polypus from a Patrice Lumumba's coup d'état viewpoint. In the case of Lumumba's overthrow, he was acting in a defensive manner preventing Her Majesty's tentacles from sinking deep into the Democratic Republic of Congo's political vitality. He was the one whose "nationalistic" overtones became an impediment to the British government successful preying on the Democratic Republic of Congo. He was preventing Her Majesty's government from absorbing the resources (nutrients) she needed from the Democratic Republic of Congo's territories in a very Machiavellian principle like manner. One can argue that the Old Kingdoms of Europe were involved in the schemes to undo the United States; however, one has to be careful not to come to quick conclusions on this fact. The only old kingdoms of Europe in existence today are Britain, Germany, Spain, France, Rome, and Russia (former USSR; the former Soviet Empire). Is it possible that they had lured the United States government into a war (the Second World War) just to entrap her and use her resources? I greatly doubt it because the war between Britain and Germany destroys anything that can support the theory. Will Nazi Germany sacrifice that much blood just to lure the United States into a war? The answer is 'No'. They can't afford to that if there wasn't some legitimate goal to do so and which in this case was to expand the Germanic Empire. Now comes the tricky question; Did Her Majesty's government lure Germany into a war just to entrap the United States? The answer is also a 'yes'. She would do this if she were playing a kind of chess game of domination and if she had legitimate reasons to believe that the United States will come to her aid if she were distressed. The author believes that Her Majesty's government was basically testing waters of entrapping the United States, when she went to war with Germany for the first time (the First World War). If the reader doesn't believe that the British government lured Germany into war with her just to entrap the United States government, then the author wishes to ask the reader these questions:

Why is it that she plays a "game of supremacy" and pursues global domination? Why is it that she dismantled the Soviet Empire using the United States? If the reader can answer these questions without any bias, then he will agree with the author on all the points raised. As the British monarchy may boast, "through the might of one of her greatest and richest colony, she has dominated, exploited and consolidated her gains (continues her expansion) in Africa, Latin America, Europe (the rest of Europe), Asia"; and will finally use these gains to dominate and consolidates her gains in the Northern Americas. Like a polypus, Her Majesty's Empire stretches across the globe and the United States by default happens to be part of that empire.

Empire:

To build an Empire isn't easy. The author must acknowledge Her Majesty's government for this feat because it requires great discipline, tact and sharp reflexes to do so. Building an Empire is no small task and the British monarchy has proven that they have indeed mastered the ways of nations on earth. However, care must be taken not to give much credit to Her Majesty's government, whom by now the reader will agree was very ruthless in the course of building this Empire. The removal of Lumumba as the Prime Minister of Democratic Republic of Congo and the intrigues that followed it proves and cements the point that his removal was part of the Empire building process and was indeed part of the process of consolidating Her Majesty's gains in Africa. Lumumba was just a pawn in the game; a pawn that needed to be removed. Her

Majesty's Empire didn't hesitate to remove him either. They needed the knight (the United States of America) to do so. The rest was history. The reader must notice that at the point in history when the United States declared her independence from Her Majesty's government, she took it upon herself to fix the United States. The declaration of independence greatly affected in a negative way the British government's plan for domination. It halted what would've been the greatest and fastest expansion of an Empire in man's history. This impediment was a challenge; challenge that needed to be fixed. Her Majesty's government had to go back to the war room; they had to go back to the drawing board after their last war with the United States; they had to re-strategize. The new strategy was that since brute force won't work on a rebelling colony, then shrewdness and cunning will work; and it worked. They only had to wait for the opportunities to carry out the new strategies. They had the initiative and they weren't about to lose it. They understood the task at hand perfectly. The author had argued that the Belgians weren't wise to the machinations of their fellow Europeans and what eventually happened to Belgium monarchy after the ousting of Lumumba will attest to this and is well documented for anyone who cares to know. The Belgium government till today is still mesmerized by the turn of events in the Democratic Republic of Congo against her interests. The United States government and the Belgian government took a toll on their prestige and honor in the Democratic Republic of Congo because the same people, who manipulated them into murdering Patrice Lumumba, also spread the rumors that they were the ones who had assassinated the man.

And as always, the prestige and honor of Her Majesty's Empire remained untainted.

Divide and Rule:
	The indirect divide and rule system employed by Her Majesty's government in the administration of her Empire made her very formidable. For the umpteenth time, the main motive of the "divide and rule" tactics is to find the differences amongst the subjects they rule and then exploit those differences. The system would allow Her Majesty's government to remote control the territories she seeks to exploit. The tactics of divide and rule was employed in dividing the United States government and Patrice Lumumba. The British government understood that the then United States government wouldn't tolerate any communist leanings in Africa. They also understood the eagerness

of Lumumba to help the Congolese people. They knew and understood that such eagerness may translate into desperation should they manipulate the United States and the United Nations into refusing Lumumba's requests for aid. They also knew and understood that the Belgian government would seek revenge if there were any slightest inkling that Lumumba was responsible for the massacre of white Belgians in South Kasai. It was the perfect setup and all the parties fell for the British government machinations. They also divided the government of the Democratic Republic Congo into those who supported Joseph Kasa-Vubu and Mobutu Sese Seko; and those who supported Patrice Lumumba. They capitalized on the fact that both Kasa-Vubu and Mobutu feared and envied Lumumba. They duo thought that Lumumba was too influential and powerful; and that this meant an uncertain future for them because Lumumba could relieve them of their positions at any point in time. The application of the indirect divide and rule system can also be seen in the way Her Majesty's government had controlled the African colonies through the local chiefs in the territories that belonged to them. The divide and rule system worked through British agents that caused certain events to take place under the auspices of the British government. The dividing point for the United States government and the Lumumba's administration was "communism"; and the dividing point for the Belgian government and the Lumumba's administration was "white supremacy" (the Congolese government had no audacity to oppose the Belgian government). The ability to successfully divide the players in the Lumumba affair ensured that Her Majesty's government maintained strong control over a territory that was rich with various mineral resources that will definitely aid the expansion of Her Majesty's Empire. The initial penetration of the Democratic Republic of Congo through the ousting of Patrice Lumumba allowed the British government to continue the further exploitation of (feeding on) the territories as well as the manipulation of the political life of the Democratic Republic of Congo.

Corruption:

The reader at this point is very conversant with the fact that corruption can be likened to a "nerve toxin". Another fact that the reader must take cognizance of is that the venom of the most poisonous of serpents is filled with "nerve toxins".

The octopus like the poisonous serpents has in its poison vassal a good dosage of "nerve toxin". Thus we may safely conclude that by similarity (by the fact that an octopus and a serpent contain nerve toxin) the octopus may be deemed to

be very poisonous. Anything that's poisonous has the capacity to cause fatal harm or death to what it poisons. The poisonous nature of corruption also makes it capable of causing fatal harm or death to any society that it gains entrance to. It spreads quickly to all parts of the society (like a "nerve toxin" would in a nervous system) and gradually leads to the death of the society. Moral decadence is the end product of corruption. The Lumumba overthrow throws great light on how corruption was used to oust a sitting prime minister. Anyone who carefully studied the intricacies of the ordeal that surrounded the coup d'état of 1960 which removed Patrice Lumumba must be very conversant with the fact that the United States CIA paid $100,000 (was mentioned earlier in the chapter) to Joseph Kasa-Vubu and Mobutu Sese Seko to have Lumumba murdered. This action by the United States CIA came as a result of the malign influence of the British MI6 which manipulated how the United States CIA perceived Lumumba. The monies paid to Kasa-Vubu (the president) and Mobutu (the chief of staff) of the Democratic Republic of Congo by the United States CIA was a bribe; a bribe that was given to murder a man (an assassination fee). The reader must have understood at this junction, that the United States CIA was very corrupt at that point in history. The corruption came in through the British government that led the United States government into believing that "foreign policy by covert action" was a better option than diplomacy. Covert action is secretive in nature; and the reader will agree with the author that most things that are often done in secret are vile. One can argue that the only way to have defeated communism was by covert action; but the assertion is a tricky one. If the United States government had allowed communism to thrive in Eastern Europe, is it remotely possible that the Soviet Union would've brought communism to the doorsteps of the United States. It's highly improbable that would have happened especially since the Soviet Union considered how equally matched both countries were on paper in terms of arms. The truth remains that "communism" would have had little or no impact on the United States. It would've only impacted Europe. The truth also remains that by simple diplomacy and education the United States government would've influenced the world into buying the idea of democracy and constitutionalism. The best option would've been for the United States government to have remained neutral in the affairs between European countries. This would've been the wisest thing to do. Unfortunately, she chose to entangle herself with Her Majesty's government and subsequently became a victim of the machinations of an expanding empire. The activities of the United States CIA and the Belgian government in the Democratic Republic of Congo which were very visible to all created the fertile ground for the thriving corruption in the Democratic Republic of Congo today. This was exactly what Her Majesty's government wanted and that's what it achieved.

Analysis of the 1953 Iranian Coup that Ousted Mohammad Mosaddeq – Chapter Thirteen

The 1953 Iranian coup d'état was the first of coup d'états the United States government took part in right after the Second World War and during peacetime. It was the first taste of "covert action" post-World War II for the United States CIA. It was the first exhibition of the control and manipulation of the foreign policy of the United States government by Her Majesty's government post-World War II. The coup d'état was carried out to depose Mohammad Mossadeq, the then prime minister of Iran. The coup took place on the 19th of August, 1953 and didn't involve the immediate death of Mossadeq. The United States government was led to believe that the Mossadeq administration was highly unreliable and had communist leanings. The British government had manipulated the United States CIA into believing that Mossadeq could be easily turned into a communist because of his association with the Tudeh party (a pro-communist Iranian party). The United States government swallowed the yarn hook, line and sinker and concluded that it was time for Mossadeq to leave the corridors of power in Iran. This decision led to the overthrow of Mossadeq and the installation of Falollah Zahedi as the new prime minister. Again, our analysis shall follow the usual circuitous path that shows in full glare the predatory nature of Her Majesty's government.

Predation; Parasitism:

The Iranian coup of 1953 presents accurately all the facts that shows that the British government has been using the United States government to consolidate her gains in the globe and expand her Empire. The use of United States in this manner can be likened to the way a predator (parasite) feeds on its host (prey); the author has reiterated this so many times. The British government sunk her tentacles into the Iranian government as far back as the early 90's. She did this through pretending to be interested in drilling oil from the Iranian territories. The reader must note that prior to the 1953 coup, the British government used the Anglo-Iranian Oil Company (secondary host) to penetrate the Iranian government. When Mossadeq nationalized the British Petroleum assets in 1952 in Iran, the going got tougher for the Empire and the

British government saw Mossadeq as a hindrance to a free flow of oil to Her Majesty's Empire. Mossadeq had to be removed immediately. The British government always finds a way to make her hosts adjust structurally to her predation; and Iran was no exception. When they discovered that the penetration through Anglo-Iranian Oil Company was no longer enough, they sought another secondary host that would complement the former secondary host (like the United States government did for the Belgian government in the coup d'état that ousted Patrice Lumumba). Through the United States government the British government sunk her tentacles (drilling a bore like the octopus would do) into Iran to complement the initial bore through the Anglo-Iranian Oil Company. When this was accomplished, the Iranian government became structurally adjusted to the whims and caprices of Her Majesty's government. As always, the United States government became weaker while Her Majesty's government became stronger.

Camouflage:

The British government hid her real reasons from the United States government as to the real purpose the coup d'etat was serving. Initially, the United States government felt that Mossadeq was the right man for the Iranian people because of his public anti-communist stance. But by sleight of wit and illusion of events, Her Majesty's government was able to manipulate the United States government into believing that Mosaddeq would turn communist at any given chance. One can argue that "nationalism" was what the British government was fighting in Iran and it was the main reason why they sought to remove

Mossadeq who was a staunch nationalist. The problem with the argument is that it's short-sighted. If nationalism was the target of Her Majesty's government attacks in the globe, then why did it seek to depose non-nationalist governments like that of Ngo Dinh Diem? The truth remains that the British government seeks to install corrupt leaders in the territories where they exploit; and the corruption in those territories led to the domination of the government of those territories and finally to their unabated exploitation. As always, Her Majesty's government finds it a lot easier to control and manipulate corrupt governments; the reason to this assertion is numerous and the reader will only do himself some good by pondering on it. "The Anti-nationalism" mantra of Her Majesty's Empire is only but a smoke screen which acts as an impediment to seeing the real picture that depicts the reasons why the series of coup d'etat orchestrated by the British government in history took place. Her Majesty's Empire seeks global domination and the rapid expansion of her empire and that's why she has controlled and manipulated the United States government into consolidating her gains in the regions where she sought dominance. That's why she never bated an eye when she sold the "increasingly ease of turning to communism" and "radical socialist land reform" Mossadeq stories to the United States CIA and cleverly hid their motives in plain sight.

Mimicry:

The author has hammered with constancy that appearances can be very deceiving; a wise and simple instruction which the United States government didn't heed to when she dealt with the British government. The United States CIA didn't keep to the simple law of "being true to one's nature". By nature, the duty of United States CIA was to gather foreign intelligence and analyze it. Quite simple right?. It isn't in the nature of the United States CIA (an intelligence gathering body to) to carry out "covert action". The role of "covert action" given to the United States CIA was done out of context and was definitely given to them under the control and manipulation of the British government. The duty of gathering foreign intelligence for the United States government remained the only priority of the United States CIA. Anything short or more of that destroys (corrupts) the nature of the United States CIA; the British government understood this and used it effectively in manipulating the United States CIA to take on the duty of a "covert actor"; she also understood that she will be undermining the real nature of the organization if she did so. The fact that the United States CIA played an active role in the ousting of Mossadeq is an open secret. The declassified documents released by the United States CIA clearly support the fact that they were the major actors in the overthrow of Mohammad Mossadeq. Her Majesty's government appeared to be the convener and propagator of anything "anti-communist" to the United States government. They appeared to be the purveyors of "freedom and democracy" to the United States government; the aim being to weaken the suspicion of the United States government. The reader must also remember that the United States government and the

British government had fought side by side during the Second World War. Who wouldn't trust a comrade? The camaraderie between the United States government and the British government after the Second World War made the United States government to see everything the British government presented to her that didn't represent the ideologies of her republic as a threat that should be eliminated. The United States government simply continued in war mode under the strict control and manipulations of Her Majesty's government based on the fears that there was always a threat out there that should be met with aggression. It would've been difficult for even the angels to convince them otherwise. Her Majesty's government understood this and capitalized massively on it. One can argue that it was the race for nuclear weapons that caused the hysteria and paranoia that prevented the United States government from the seeing that she was being maligned by the British government. That argument is half truth. Why? If the United States government sought to develop nuclear weapons, she would've accomplished such a feat using simple intelligence gathering. There was no need of the "covert action"stuff. What was needed was the ability to know what the competitor was doing as pertains to the development of nuclear weapons; quite simple right? The nuclear weapon arms race only magnified the communist and socialist threats. Communism and socialism were smoke screens that gave Her Majesty's government an appearance of conjugal and mutual feelings with the United States government.

Octopus; Polypus:

The distinguishing fact about the Iranian affair was that the United States government was not involved the first time in the penetration of the Iranian administration. Her Majesty's government sunk a tentacle into the Iranian government using the Anglo-Iranian Oil Company. The United States government had not come into the scene as at then (prior to the Second World War). The tentacles of Her Majesty's Empire didn't fail to reach the Iranian territories in her quest for domination. The vitality to be gained from penetrating the territories of Iran that were very rich in oil and gas was too tempting for the British government. The United States government through helping depose Mossadeq, only aided the further expansion of Her Majesty's Empire and the consolidation of her gains in the Middle East. The Middle East is so vital to the British government that in her game of chess, she didn't mind using the United States government as a knight to destabilize governments that she felt will act as an impediment to the her imperialism. The author has reiterated times without number that Her Majesty's government prefers corrupt administrations in power because it allows her to easily control and manipulate such an administration as well as gain unfettered access to the resources (nutrients) of the territories where those governments preside. The Mossadeq saga shows how Her Majesty's government through divide and rule tactics forced the shells of the Mossadeq administration apart. It also reveals how quickly the Mossadeq administration became poisoned when the United States CIA money started changing hands amongst the key

Iranian power-brokers. The Iranian power-brokers who were once loyal to Mossadeq became very hostile to him because of the poison of corruption. The United States government was made to be a secondary host that was used to sap the rich oil and gas deposits of the Iranian administration which was in this case a primary host. Immediately the Iranian government became structurally adjusted to the whims and caprices of Her Majesty's government through the United States CIA "covert actions" on its government, it became very easy to exploit her. Mossadeq was only a pawn in the game and so was anyone who the British government kept in power after the ousting of Mossadeq. After Mossadeq was removed, the British government continued her drilling of the Iranian oil and gas as a result of the changes made in her favor by the newly installed government, which she controlled, thereby leading to her gaining of unfettered access to the Iranian resources she desired. By using the United States government to accomplish this feat, Her Majesty's government maintained once again her prestige and honor while the United States government became weaker and much hated in Iran and the Middle East.

Empire:

To build an empire isn't a day job. The British government understood this fundamental fact. The octopus kills its prey in a "slow" but effective manner. The truth is, to build an empire requires patience; a patience which Her Majesty's government has shown to have in abundance. Like a vulture, the British government waits for the various governments which she manipulates and controls to decay by corruption before she comes in to feed on them. The reader must also observe that the central themes of the modus operandi of the British government are domination and exploitation by the "shearing force of divide and rule"; and the "poison of corruption". These important themes of Her Majesty's government were constantly employed in the control and manipulations of the United States government by the British government. The Mossadeq affair is no stranger to this either. Like most leaders of the various nations whom we've seen were ousted by the machinations of the British government, Mossadeq wasn't privy to the fact that his activities were an impediment to the expansion of Her Majesty's empire. They were ignorant of the British government quest for dominating the globe and setting a new world order which solely benefitted Her Majesty's government. Mossadeq was very unaware of the fact that he was only but "a pawn in a game played by an octopus". The successful control and manipulation of the United States government by the British government was clearly seen in her desire to remove a democratically elected Mossadeq because the British government made her believe it was the right thing to do. The failure of the United States CIA to independently analyze the real situation in Iran was her undoing. If the United States government had monitored the situations in Iran, she would've been very aware of the machinations of Her Majesty's government and would've refused to be a willing tool in the hands of the British government. The independence of the United States secret intelligence capabilities was destroyed when she decided that it was okay for the immature and inexperienced Office of Strategic Services (OSS) to take over the mantle of foreign intelligence gathering from the United States Secret Service. The United States Secret Service would've been more than enough to gather the necessary foreign intelligence required by the United States government for her security because she has more experience in that area than even the United States military. The United States CIA dependence on the British MI6 for "actionable intelligence" made it possible for her to come under the strong influence of the whims and caprices of Her Majesty's government; it also led to the unhindered progression of the expansion of Her Majesty's Empire as well as the consolidation of her gains in the Middle East as seen in the Mossadeq overthrow.

Divide and Rule:
The author is yet to see a government so masterful in the art of divide and rule like the British government. They are the real dons of this art of dividing societies along their lines of disagreement. The British government is very good at making the people of the territories where they seek to exploit and sap bicker on and fight over their differences. The aim of expanding these differences amongst the people is to enable Her Majesty's government maintain her control and manipulation over them. The Mossadeq ousting allows us to see the mastership of the British government in the art of divide and rule. The luring of the United States CIA into the Mossadeq affair was carried out by pure divide and rule

tactics. The British government understood that the United States government will differ with anyone on the basis of "communism or socialism". Her Majesty's government also understood clearly that to create the dividing point between the United States government and the Mossadeq administration, all she needed to do, was to convince the United States CIA that Mossadeq would turn a communist with little or no pressure from the Tudeh party. The United States government believed the yarn when it was sold to them. The United States fearful and bitter hate for the ideologies of "communism" and "socialism" made this possible as well as the fear of domination and destruction by the Soviets. The United States government thought that the enemy was far away whereas the enemy was closer than he could ever imagine. The Mossadeq government was as well divided by the United States CIA using very slandering propaganda and bribes. The Iranian Shah as at then, was made to believe that Mossadeq sought exclusive powers and that he was about to be deposed and made irrelevant in government by Mossadeq. This angered the Shah and he held grudges against Mossadeq which multiplied when he signed the two royal decrees which removed Mohammad Mossadeq and installed Fazlollah Zahedi. The $1,000,000 provided by Allen Dulles (the then United States CIA Chief) was used to bribe the Iranian parliament, the news media, the powerful families in Iran and all the major criminal gang networks in Iran to turn and work against Mossadeq. Mossadeq never knew what he had been up against even until his death. The statement he made after his arrest in 1953 proves this. He assumed that he was battling the forces that were against "constitutionalism" not realizing that the forces which were against him sought to dominate the globe and not even a Mossadeq was going to stop them. The United States government never realized that she was also being controlled and manipulated by Her Majesty's government in the Mossadeq affair; and neither did the other principal actors in the coup d'état realize that they were just suckers.

Corruption:
When a society is poisoned by corruption, it means that the society dies a natural death and remains dead regardless of how much its people think that such a society is alive. Corruption is a very terrible killer of

good governance. One of the prominent features of good governance is that it's open and transparent. Corruption doesn't permit openness or transparency. Anything done in secret has the greatest tendency to become corrupt. Nothing illegal or immoral is usually done in the open. Most illegal or immoral things are done in the secret and are best kept secret. That's why the best form of governance is an open one. The author has reiterated in the previous chapters that the United States government was corrupted when she adopted the "foreign policy by covert action". The moment the United States government towed the line of "foreign policy by covert action", it gradually derailed and became a "secret government". The secrecy of the immoral and illegal "covert action" by the United States government meant that she entirely dropped the "foreign policy by diplomacy and commerce" designed for her by the framers. She saw her "diplomacy and commerce" as instruments to be only used for nations that didn't threaten to become "communist or socialist". It's obvious that communism and socialism don't belong to the fundamental ideologies of the United States government and her people; who believe in democracy, commerce and freedom. However, the mistake made by the United States government in fighting communism and socialism is that it never pondered on the fact that ideologies aren't changed by "covert action". The truth remains that the United States government succeeded in dismantling the former Soviet Union, but it didn't succeed in destroying the ideology of "communism and socialism". This is very clear in the simple fact that Russia, North Korea and China are still communist countries. The cold war dismantled "communist and socialist" states but didn't dismantle the ideology. To defeat an ideology requires more than just assassinations, black political propaganda, economic sabotage, etc. It requires more than all that. To effectively get rid of an ideology from a society, one must carry out a gradual "psychological reconfiguration" that aims to scrub off the ideology. This "psychological reconfiguration" isn't your everyday military psychological operation or political propaganda. No, it isn't. Removing an existing ideology requires a very deep psychological work. That's exactly what the United States failed to understand and it led to her exposure to the whims and caprices of the British government and eventually to the total control and manipulation of the United States government by Her

Majesty's government. The British government understood these facts (that is the nature of ideologies); she also understood that she would be sending the United States government on wild goose chase if she made her fight ideological based wars just like the United States did in other parts of the Middle East later in her history (the British government manipulated the nations of the Middle East to believe that the United States government was fighting Islam). For the umpteenth time, the British Empire's formula of "ideological based division" always works. The Mossadeq affair was no different. Mossadeq's administration was tumbled inside out using the poison of corruption. Allen Dulles, the United States CIA Chief at the time of the coup d'état released $1,000,000 for the bribing (corruption) of the major power-brokers in Iran at the time of the coup d'etat. The reader by now understands that Dulles was basically dancing to the tunes of Her Majesty's government by bribing the Iranian power-brokers. He was basically chasing the wind; the wind of fighting the ideology of "communism and socialism". If only Dulles, had understood that he was chasing shadows, he would have retraced his steps. When United States CIA money changed hands in Iran, the United States government acted as exactly a host would act when a parasite feeds on it. She simply gave up her vitality (the financial resource amounting to $1,000,000) for the usage of Her Majesty's government. As always, the United States grew weaker while the British government grew stronger.

Analyzing the 1954 Guatemalan Coup that Ousted Jacob Arbenz – Chapter Fourteen

The removal of Jacob Arbenz by the United States CIA as the leader of the Guatemalan government was the highlight of the year 1954 in international politics. Arbenz was ousted from power on 27th June, 1954 and replaced with Carlos Castillo Armas. The overthrow of Arbenz reinforced the United States weakness for fighting ideologies using "brute force"; a weakness which was greatly exploited by Her Majesty's government. The United States government saw the Arbenz administration as a communist regime capable of diminishing her pro-democracy influence in the Latin Americas. The chapter will analyze the Arbenz affair from the viewpoints used in the previous chapters, the aim being that the author wants to maintain a degree of uniformity which allows the reader to see Her Majesty's government through the lens of a master manipulator who uses the "sleight of wit" and the "illusion of events" to strongly control and manipulate United States government.

Predation; Parasitism:

The Arbenz affair brings to light another masterpiece control and manipulation of the United States government by the British government. The Arbenz saga portrays the typical Her Majesty's government attitude towards the nations she relates with. Her Majesty's government structurally adjusted United States government the secondary host to act in a manner that ensured that the Guatemalan government the primary host met her nutritional needs. The British government continued its predation on the Guatemalan government through the United States government who was manipulated into believing that the Arbenz government were leaning towards "communism". One can argue that the United States government was "predisposed" to fight communism during the Cold War. However, one must be careful not to forget that the fight against communism didn't start until the Second World War had ended. The Second World War was a war against the Nazis. The United States government saw "communism" as the greatest threat as at then and even today because she interpreted communism as being associated with a potential "nuclear threat" from the former Soviet Union. It was an exaggerated or magnified interpretation of communism. She couldn't mentally separate the "nuclear arm race" from the ideology of "communism". The important question now is, who sold the "exaggerated communism" threat idea to the United States government? This answer to the question is very simple; it was the British government through the British MI6. The reader must remember that Her Majesty's government manipulated the United States government into creating the United States CIA modeled after the British MI6. This move created a sought of magical "mirror effect", where the United States CIA saw itself as the British MI6. Therefore, whatever the British MI6 did, the United

States CIA sought to do. Therefore, the United States CIA due to this "mirror effect" was bound to perceive "actionable intelligence" the same way the British MI6 would. So, if the British MI6 saw communism as a threat (the Soviet Empire stood in the way of Her Majesty's global domination), the United States CIA (the brain and eyes of the United States government) would definitely see communism in that light. The "predisposition to communism" argument doesn't explain accurately what led the United States government to see "communism" as much of a bigger threat than the British government "imperialism". The truth is prior to World War II; the United States government stance on British government imperialism was hardliner. The United States government right from the day she declared her independence always saw Her Majesty's government imperialism as tyrannical and vile. However, after the Second World War (the British-German War; which was engineered to entrap the United States government?), the United States government perception of the British government changed due to Her Majesty's government use of the manipulative "sleight of wit" and "illusion of events" on her. This change in perception brought to what was a relatively peaceful republic since its formation, so much pains and sorrows over the years after the Second World War. For emphasis sake, the United States government was manipulated into becoming Her Majesty's Empire knight, like a knight, the United States government has been fighting wars since the aftermath of the World War II to the benefit of the British government. Nature has made it possible for any predator to always hold on tight to the vitality it gains from the prey. The parasitic relationship between the British government and the United States government is no different. In the quest for the expansion of her Empire and the domination of the world, Her Majesty's government has preyed upon the United States government and held on to it "very" tight.

Camouflage:

Long before the United States government came into the Abernz affair, the British government had issues with Abernz's predecessor. Abernz's predecessor had strong "anti-colonial" sentiments which Her Majesty's government didn't favor. It happened that at one time in history, Guatamela was a British government's colony. The British government also had farms in the Guatamelan colony, which provided ample supply of fruits to Her Majesty's Empire. During the

Guaatamelan revolution, the British government discovered that she was fast losing its grip on a territory that provided an important share of the Empire's fruit supply. She needed to act fast in order to regain her grip on Guatemala. The reader must understand that the United States government opinion on the British-Guatemala affair before Abernz took power from his predecessor was entirely against the British government's colonialist tendencies in Guatemala. What caused the sudden change in attitude of the United States government (who despite her initial anti-colonialism stance towards Guatemala; and despite the fact that the British government had labeled the Guatemalan government as "communist") didn't compromise on their hardliner? The answer to that question lies partly in the premise of camouflage. The British government prior to the ousting of Arbenz had always maintained that the Arbenz predecessor was an "anti-colonialist" and a "communist". However, when Arbenz took power they said that Arbenz was "only making socialist reforms" and wasn't a "communist". The reader must do well to notice the sudden change in perception. Why the sudden reversal in the labeling of the Guatemalan administration especially if you considered that Arbenz was his predecessor's right hand man and continued with the reforms he initiated? The answer is that 'the British government didn't want the United States government especially the Dulles Brother's and the United States CIA to believe that they were framing Jacob Arbenz into a communist'. There is no other reason for that behavior. If the United States CIA had suspected that the British MI6 was framing Arbenz, it would have damaged a new relationship and led to the discovery of the various controlling and manipulative practices Her Majesty's government towards the control and manipulation of the United States government. All hell would've let loose. No discovery was made and Her Majesty's government dominance continued. The ability of the British MI6 to hide her real intentions towards Guatemala allowed her to strengthen her grip on the Guatemalan territories and consolidate her gains in the Latin Americas. The United States government was controlled and manipulated into helping her achieve this purpose. Camouflage was employed by Her Majesty's government in the Arbenz saga. The so called unseen "Abernz enemies" trying to paint him as a "communist" were in fact Guatemalans working for the British MI6 and lobbyists in the United States paid to work on behalf of Her Majesty's government. If the Dulles brothers were alive today and were told that they were manipulated into believing that Abernz was a "communist", they wouldn't believe it for what it's worth. Her Majesty's government hid the fact that the Abernz ousting was indeed a mission to expand her Empire.

Mimicry:

Despite hiding their real intentions for controlling and manipulating the United States government into removing Abernz from power, the British government also appeared to be very concerned about "communist" influences in the regions where she sought to consolidate her gains by using the vitality of the United States government. She also appeared to be actively engaged in the battle against "communism or socialism" whereas her real intentions were the domination and exploitation of the territories where she had sunk her tentacles. The appearance of "common strategic objectives" feigned by Her Majesty's Empire was done to throw the United States government off guard; and it did throw them off guard. If the British government was really bent on fighting communism and socialism like she appeared to the United States to be doing, she wouldn't have waited for the United States to take the lead on the fight against communism; she would've been at the forefront of the various "covert actions" carried out by the United States government without needing the help of the United States government. For the British government, her so called fight against "communism" ended up only in passing "actionable intelligence" to the United States CIA and the "planning of the coup d'état" to oust the "pawns" they saw as threats to Her Majesty's imperialism and global dominance. There was barely any contribution of resources whatsoever in the execution of the coup d'état that removed Arbenz from power. This fact exemplifies the "parasitic" relationship that exists between the British government and the United States government. One can argue that Her Majesty's government didn't have ample resources to cater for the coup d'état. Though it may be termed a valid argument, the truth remains that the sums of monies used for the coup d'état were very minute when compared to the overall size of the British government's budget. There was certainly the economic factor in the reasons why the British government never actively participated in the coup d'état; but it was only secondary. Another good argument can be that the British government sought to preserve the prestige and honor of Her Majesty's government when she made the United States government execute the coup d'état using her personnel and resources; this reason is also secondary. The main reason why Her Majesty's government sought to feign the appearance of fighting "communism" was that she wanted to douse any form of suspicion the United States government could want to entertain about her real intentions. The United States government was finally suckered into Her Majesty's government schemes for global domination, when the British government began the so called process of the "decolonization" of her territories. This was the final nail in the coffin of the United States government and any form of suspicion she might have had about the British government intention towards imperialism disappeared. Nevertheless, if the reader took out time to study the colonial territories that were granted independence by Her Majesty's government, the reader shall indeed discover that the British government maintained a very stronghold over the areas that were deemed to be independent. The hegemony of the British Empire over the so called "decolonized territories" continued despite the form or appearance of independency of the territories. The United States government at the junction when the British government granted independence to her colonial territories, totally took its eyes off the "imperialism" of Her Majesty's Empire and focused on the exaggerated threat of "communism or socialism" (exaggerated by the nuclear arms race; the United States government couldn't remove or change or control its outcomes of the ideologies it fought).

Octopus; Polypus:

Assuredly, the reader can understand at this point, that wherever Her Majesty's government had sunk her tentacles, she wouldn't relinquish such a place on a platter of gold. The British government will never relinquish any of her territories without a fight. This is a simple fact which the United States government and the government of those territories where Her Majesty's government had sunk her tentacles failed to understand. The game played by Her Majesty's government in the ousting of Jacob Arbenz, was a game played in the other territories where the British government needed to strengthen her grip on the administration of the government of those territories as well as consolidate her gains in such a region where the territories existed. Arbenz was only but a pawn in the game of world domination. The nature of a polypus (the multi-tentacle) makes it a perfect multi-feeder. The polypus can feed on multiple preys at a time. It was created to behave that way. Her Majesty's government has modeled itself to behave in the same manner that a polypus will behave. She is a multi-feeder too; basically feeding on the resources of other nations through structurally adjusting the government of those nations to her whims and caprices. Inadvertently, the British government has preyed upon the United States government and turned her into a perfect secondary prey (host) through which she saps the vitality of other nations. The United States not being privy to this knowledge, has allowed herself to be used in such a manner that benefits

Her Majesty's government. In the saga that follows the overthrow of Arbenz, the reader can clearly understand that much predatory behavioral mechanisms was employed by the British government to entrap the United States government into acting in her interests. Like in similar coup d'état that the United States government had executed on the control and manipulation of the British government as well as at the unwitting behest of Her Majesty's government, she had been led into believing that she was acting in her best interests. For a rapidly expanding Empire, the fruit plantations of Guatemala were too important to be left alone. One can argue that in the Arbenz coup d'état, the United States government had drawn exaggerated conclusions about the extent of communist influence among Arbenz's advisers. This argument can be valid if only we can determine the "real source" of the intelligence that made the United States government draw such exaggerated conclusions on the influence (the manipulation) of "communism" on the Arbenz administration. The truth remains that the British MI6 through her Guatemala agents and the United Fruit Company lobbyists (British MI6 agents as well) had controlled and manipulated the United States government into believing that Arbenz was a "real danger communist plant" that needed to be uprooted. The mirror effect which the British MI6 had on the United States CIA caused the United States CIA to make the ousting of Arbenz a "national security" priority; she accomplished this by sharing damning intelligence on Arbenz advisers which showed their connections with the communist bloc,. There's no denying of the fact that the British government had insisted that Arbenz was not a "communist" despite the evidences she was presenting about Arbenz advisers to the United States CIA. What this tells the reader is that Her Majesty's government needed to douse the suspicion of the United States government on the fact that she was being manipulated into thinking that Arbenz was a "communist". If the British government was very sure that Arbenz was not a "communist', why didn't they inform the Arbenz administration of the coup d'état plot to remove them from power or even sold arms to Guatemalan government to defend itself against the planned invasion of the United States CIA sponsored paramilitary mercenaries or even notify the international community of the planned invasion? Why did they compartmentalize the whole affair if not for the fact that they were controlling and manipulating the United States government into buying the yarn that Arbenz was a "communist". In the aftermath of the Arbenz overthrow, the outcomes were the same as always, the Her Majesty's government prestige and honor grew, while the hatred and angst of the United States in the Latin Americas ballooned very quickly.

Empire:

One of the characteristics of an Empire that the author had mentioned in the description of an Empire is that an empire is headed by a sole ruler. In the case of the British government which tolerates a monarchy, the Queen of England (Britain) happens to be the head of the British monarchy. If the reader reflects on what the author has written so far, he shall agree with the author that the

British government by virtue of her quest for territorial expansion and consolidation is an Empire. The key question to be asked at this point is who's the head of the British Empire? The truth is that, the head of the British Empire is the Queen of England (Britain). Even though, this is common knowledge, the author seeks to convey this common knowledge in the most logical manner. The prime minister of Britain cannot be the ruler of the British Empire because according to the British constitution, a British prime minister takes his or her orders from the Queen. The facts we've laid down so far are solemn truths. The reader can safely conclude that based on the assertions we've made so far, we can write that the Queen is an Empress. If the Empress controls an Empire, it must clearly mean that she will do whatever she deems necessary to achieve the control. The reader will also agree with the author, that so far, it has been established without doubt that the United States government was controlled and manipulated by Her Majesty's government. The key question to be asked now is who gave the order to bring the United States government under the control and manipulation of the British government? The answer is very straight forward and simple, it was the Queen who gave the permission to the British government to bring the United States government under her control; the reason being that she's the most powerful person in Britain. The aim of the author is not to vilify the Queen; not at all. The aim of clearing this doubt is to ensure that the reader has a firm grasp of the facts that pertain to an Empire. The reader must also understand that the Emperor or Empress shall always act in the best interest of his or her

Empire. This is a true statement and any misgivings about it shouldn't exist. Thus, we can safely conclude that the Queen of England (Britain) shall always act in a manner very beneficial to the British Empire and very inimical to the other nations she relates with. Therefore, we can also safely conclude that Her Majesty's government shall never act in the interest of the United States government. As an Empire, Britain would tolerate no rebellion from the nations she considers to be under her Empire and shall do anything within her powers to quash any form of rebellion that arises within her Empire. We've also established beyond reasonable doubt that the United States is considered by the British government to be under Her Majesty's Empire because the United States used to be her former colony and she won't lose her on a whim; the United States can also be found on the globe and imperialism seeks to dominate the globe; the history between the duo, always shows Her Majesty's government trying to exert some sort of influence (directly or indirectly; straightforwardly or subtly) on the United States government. For the umpteenth time, this implies that British government shall always act in a manner that's inimical to the well being of the United States and her people. The Arbenz affair proves that the United States government is indeed under the influence of Her Majesty's government control and manipulation; as well as also clearing any doubt as to the fact that the United States territories are considered to be under Her Majesty's Empire or not. The intricate and delicate nature of the narrative that followed the ousting of Arbenz makes it impossible to think otherwise. The British government interest in Guatemala was the fruits exports that she derived from the fruit plantations in Guatemala; the British government was clever enough to conceal these secondary interests from the United States government in order to douse her suspicions if there be any. Another smoke screen also employed in the overthrow of Arbenz was that of the seemingly British struggle for the Belizean territories with the Guatemalan government. It also took the eyes and thoughts of the United States government far away from the real reasons why Her Majesty's government sought to remove Arbenz from the corridors of power in Guatemala.

Divide and Rule:

To master the "divide and rule" tactics is to master the art of control and manipulation. The author has throughout the course of the book, associated "divide and rule" tactics with imperialistic leadership. The reader must understand that those who thought of the "divide and rule" tactics never saw it as sinister (despite how manipulative it is). They took cues from nature especially the octopus; the reason being that from time immemorial, kingdoms have always found it very difficult to rule their subjects in a way that accommodated all the interests of their subjects at the same time. Any good student of psychology shall indeed admit that it's very difficult to please people. The inability to please everyone meant that it was necessary for rulers to determine a way to prevent dissatisfaction from their subjects. Dissatisfaction stemmed from the inability to be pleased. The fact that majority of the subjects under a ruler were always dissatisfied meant that they could unite and overthrow a ruler. This can be clearly seen throughout the history of man and his kingdoms. This instability of kingdoms caused by the unity of subjects who weren't always satisfied with the current leadership and sought to topple them, always worried the ruler of the kingdom. The ruler went back to his or her private quarters and thought of the best way to administer control over their kingdoms. They pondered deeply on this and they discovered that the only way to solve the problem was to ensure that the subjects they ruled were never united against them. They successfully implemented this line of thought and discovered that it worked effectively. The rulers learnt to behave like the octopus; they learnt to "force the shells of their prey apart". The overthrow of the Arbenz administration definitely portrays vividly the manner in which the "divide and rule" tactics can be successfully employed. The British government was able to divide the

Arbenz administration and the United States government along the lines of "communism". Her Majesty's government sold the idea to the United States government that Jacob Arbenz was a staunch "communist". The United States CIA was controlled and manipulated into believing that Arbenz's retention of power despite being a communist and a leader of the Guatemala government meant that there was a possibility of having other Latin America nations become aligned with the communist bloc. On this basis did the United States government without further thought make it a priority to oust Arbenz. The divide and rule tactics comes to play when under the British government's control and manipulation, the United States government through the United States CIA divided Guatemala into those who were for Arbenz and those who were against Arbenz (mostly those exiled by Arbenz and

other dissidents who hated his guts).
They quickly accomplished this feat
by steering those who were against
Arbenz under the leadership of
Carlos Castillo Armas. When Arbenz
was eventually toppled, a bitter
resentment towards the United States
government spread in the Latin
Americas where the United States
government was labeled as
"imperialists. As always, the United
States government took the fall for
Her Majesty's government whose
prestige and honor remained
untainted in the Latin Americas.

Corruption:
     It will be insufficient to discuss
corruption in the Arbenz affair,
without discussing the role played by
the Dulles brothers in the whole
affair. The Dulles brothers (John
Dulles and Allen Dulles) were both
instrumental in the removal of the
Jacob Arbenz from power in

Guatemala. The Dulles brothers had strong ties to the United Fruit Company and this factored in strongly in their desire to have Arbenz removed by "covert action". One can argue that the "foreign policy by covert action" corrupted the Dulles brothers. This is a solid argument, if you considered that the Dulles brothers both occupied important positions in government during this period in history. John Dulles was secretary of state and Allen Dulles was the United States CIA Chief. The key question that pops up is this; did the Dulles brothers use their positions to protect their interests in the United Fruit Company? The answer to the question is 'yes', they had used their positions to influence the outcome of the approval to use "covert paramilitary action" on the Arbenz administration. This was a total conflict of interests according to the laws of the United States; the move bespoke of massive corruption at the highest levels of the United States government at that time in history. However, "foreign policy by covert action" made it okay for the Dulles brothers to have gotten away with such an "abuse of office while in government". The absolute power bestowed upon the Dulles brothers by the "foreign policy by covert action" corrupted them absolutely. Allen Dulles had signed off over $5,000,000 of the United States CIA for the operation to oust Arbenz. By acting in such a manner, the United States government confirmed that it was a host of the British government and was indeed using her resources (vitality) to nourish Her Majesty's government. The monies used in Operation Success (the name of the United States CIA controlled operation that removed Arbenz from office) were equally used in a corrupt manner amongst the enemies of Arbenz. The monies given to Armas to spearhead the coup d'état were hugely unaccounted for. Most of it went into private pockets. The corruption by stealth was craftily employed by the British government to weaken the United States government. The poison of corruption is a very potent weapon in the destruction of powerful Republics or Empires. The enemies of Roman Republic had used the poison of corruption on the Roman Republic and her senate. It led to the quick deterioration of the Roman Republic and eventually the collapse of her Empire. Corruption when effectively used can weaken nations; the British government thoroughly understood this fact. The poison of corruption eats deep into the fabrics of any society where it is injected in. It causes a rot in the collective psyche of the people. The people making up a corrupt society no longer see immorality or illegality as wrong. They embrace lawlessness and reject righteousness. Such a society grows weaker by the day and eventually dies. Corruption makes them unable to defend themselves from attacks by external enemies. When attacked, they collapse quickly like a pack of cards. Like the octopus weakens its prey through nerve toxins, corruption weakens any family, clan, tribe, nation and continent where it penetrates. Corruption is the major hindrance to the development and progress of societies. Corruption turns humans into sub-humans. Corruption destroys and destroys completely. Her Majesty's government having also mastered this principle; has used it aggressively to weaken the governments they seek to dominate.

Conclusions; A New United States Foreign Policy? – Chapter Fifteen

Most nations on earth sheared apart by divide and rule as well as poisoned with corruption of Her Majesty's Empire are very much dead as the author writes. These nations have died a natural death because that is the end game of every predation. Predation always leaves the prey dead because once the vitality of an organism is sapped, death follows quickly. It seems however that the United States government's survival of the onslaught of Her Majesty's Empire whims and caprices shows that it has an antidote to the shearing apart by divide and rule as well as poison by corruption employed by her. It is very easy to pinpoint what this antidote is. One can argue that it's the democracy of the United States government that has kept it going so far despite her purposeful maligning by the British government. The argument is only okay if you saw democracy as a representative form of government. But the Old Roman Republic was running a representative form of government and despite that she still collapsed. The Old Roman Republic had a Senate. The same with those nations of the earth whose government is dead due to the maligning activities of Her Majesty's Empire in the territories of those nations. So, the representative government argument doesn't cut it. Representative government doesn't stop the divide and rule tactics from being employed in any tier and arm of government whatsoever. It doesn't stop it at all. Representative government doesn't also stop the poison of corruption. A representative government that gets injected with the poison of corruption quickly dies a natural death because corruption as the author reiterated severally, spreads like wild fire. Corruption like any nerve toxin hampers the firing of governmental processes in all the arms and tiers of government. When this happens, the representative government becomes stagnant and unproductive. Like any sick man or woman bound to die, such a representative government begins to die a natural death by first sinking into oblivion. This is what has happened to representative governments of the many territories where Her Majesty's Empire has sunk her tentacles into. The reader can therefore see for himself or herself that the representative government isn't enough to stop the shearing apart by divide and rule as well as the poison of corruption.

Therefore, we cannot attribute the United States government survival of Her Majesty's government's onslaught till date to just "democracy". It goes beyond that. The natural immunity of the United States government lies in her "Constitution".

It's very important that the reader understands that the framers of the United States "Constitution" knew what they were doing. The founders of the United States Republic as we know it today were mainly Europeans who were privy to the whims and caprices of the monarchs of Europe. They understood that shearing apart by divide and rule can be employed in the destabilization of government (democratic or non-democratic); they also firmly understood that the poison of corruption can be injected into the government to cause the death of governance. They were very wise men who had learnt a lot from their experiences in Europe. They were no fools either. They understood that the British monarchy would do anything in her powers to bring the United States government under it. They were knowledgeable in all these. They therefore sought natural laws that will make the United States government "immune" to the whims and caprices of Europe. The United States Constitution framers saw the United States as an individual. The bodily "constitution" of an individual if weak, will make him prone to diseases and sickness. However, an individual with a strong constitution will survive even the harshest of diseases and sicknesses. These, they also clearly understood. They, thus applied this principle of "immunity" to government. A government with a weak constitution will fall apart when met with deadly external influence. Nevertheless, a government with a strong constitution will by virtue of its "immunity" survive even the most deadly of external influences. They also discovered that no government had "natural immunity". They discovered that the only way to secure government from malign influences was was to give it "immunity" through a "strong" constitution. The key question now is what did the framers or the founders of the United States Republic see as a "strong" constitution? Did they see a constitution that promoted "freedom" as a strong constitution? 'Not really'. The framers knew that if they built the United States constitution on "freedom" alone, it could easily be usurped by individuals who don't believe in "freedom". If "freedom" was the rallying point of the United States government, then she won't have survived Her Majesty's onslaught for long. Freedom was only but a part of the reason why the

United States constitution is "strong". If as an individual, I knew that I was free to do so, so and so, I became knowledgeable to what I can or can't do. So does Mr. X, Mr. Y and Mr. Z who are individuals like me.

The framers understood that "knowing and understanding" your rights as an individual made you see others individuals as your "equals". "Equality" was the foundation of the United States constitution. Wherever equality thrived, injustice disappeared. The reader must take note of this. According to the founders of the United States of America, not knowing your rights meant not knowing that you we were all created equally by the Creator. It meant that an individual can be treated in an unjust manner by another individual and deem it okay because he doesn't understand that he was "equal" to the other individual who was meting injustice to him. The founders of the United States Republic also understood that the reason for this equality lies in the fact that all men share the same nature. That is, all men created have individual bodies and have the capacity to nurture individual thoughts. The "equality" of individuals laid the foundation for the modern United States Republic as we know it today. Justice naturally accompanied equality. Wherever, inequality existed, the ugly head of injustice will rise. The framers thoroughly understood this as well. Justice is guaranteed by the United States constitution because all Americans are deemed equal. A Senator in the United States Republic who earned hundreds of thousands of dollars a year was deemed no different from a man who had a minimum wage paying job. They were deemed equal not only before the law, but before the Creator. If an American was offended or hurt or murdered by another America, he (or any party that represents him) will seek justice in the court of law on the presumption that he is equal to the other individual who had caused damage. "Equality" served as an antidote (a strong immunity) to shearing apart by divide and rule as well as the poison of corruption. Why? Let's look at it this way; even if you divided a society or its government whose constitution is built on equality, based on the glaring differences they've amongst themselves, the "sense of equality" exuded by the constitution they possess remains a strong natural force that'll always bring them together. Thus, the framers understood that equality through the constitution was always going to be a rallying point for the United States government and her people. That's why the United States government and her people must protect their constitution with their last blood and ensure that through a "foreign policy by constitutionalism" they export equality to the entire globe. This was the dreams and aspirations of the founders of the United States Republic.

What's "foreign policy by constitutionalism"? The "foreign policy by constitutionalism" means that the United States government through her powers and influence should make other nations of the world adopt "exactly" the same constitution as hers. Once again, this is can be viewed as a divine mandate that must be achieved by the United States to ensure that life is injected into most nations of the world that have died a natural death due to the forces of divide and rule as well as corruption. This is the only form of sacrifice accepted by United States founders. The "foreign policy by constitutionalism" allows the United States government to spread freedom like a wildfire. It also allows the United States government to replicate itself in other parts of the world. Imagine the amount of healing this foreign policy strategy will bring to the world. A "foreign policy by constitutionalism" ensures that the basic freedoms and values of democracy the United States government seeks to promote in the world is achieved without glitches. This "foreign policy of constitutionalism" will ensure that the United States Republic consolidates the gains of her "magical" constitution that continually upholds the tenets of liberty, equality and justice. The "foreign policy by constitutionalism" will ensure that the United States government by the virtue of her benevolence creates a world that breeds peace. Another key question that arises is this, how do you make nations buy into the "foreign policy by constitutionalism" without coercion? The answer is very clear and simple. You spread the "foreign policy by constitutionalism" using the method of "psychological reconfiguration". The psychological reconfiguration has an educational component to it. This educational aspect of this method allows the United States government to sensitize the various nations where her influence reaches to adopt a replica constitution like that of the United States government. The "psychological reconfiguration" may or may not be used in the furtherance of the objective of "foreign policy by constitutionalism". The psychological reconfiguration must be applied with tact. However, the advantages of using psychological reconfiguration to achieve the foreign policy goals lies in the fact that it's very effective and works within a reasonable time frame.

The United States government constitution was created to ideally promote "free trade" through equality. This was the main idea behind the mantra of "prosperity by commerce" promulgated by the founders of the United States Republic. The United States government must through its commercial relations with other nations of the world influence them into adopting an exact copy or replica of the "constitution" of the United States government. An adoption of the exact copy or replica of the United States constitution by other nations of the world will engender

the peace, harmony and love the
world clearly needs.

The End.